Logan Cave National Wildlife Refuge

Comprehensive Conservation Plan

**U.S. Department of the Interior
Fish and Wildlife Service
Southeast Region**

August 2008

Submitted by: _____ Date: 7/3/2008
Durwin Carter, Refuge Manager
Holla Bend NWR

Concur: _____ Date: 8/1/08
Ricky Ingram, Refuge Supervisor
Southeast Region

Concur: _____ Date: 8-6-08
Jon Andrew, Regional Chief
Southeast Region

Approved by: _____ Date: 8/8/08
Sam Hamilton, Regional Director
Southeast Region

COMPREHENSIVE CONSERVATION PLAN

LOGAN CAVE NATIONAL WILDLIFE REFUGE

Benton County, Arkansas

U.S. Department of the Interior
Fish and Wildlife Service

Southeast Region
Atlanta, Georgia

August 2008

TABLE OF CONTENTS

COMPREHENSIVE CONSERVATION PLAN

LIST OF FIGURES

LIST OF TABLES

Executive Summary

The Fish and Wildlife Service has prepared this Comprehensive Conservation Plan (CCP) to guide the management of Logan Cave National Wildlife Refuge (Logan Cave NWR) in Benton County, Arkansas. The CCP outlines programs and corresponding resource needs for the next 15 years, as mandated by the National Wildlife Refuge System Improvement Act of 1997 (Improvement Act).

Public involvement in the development of the Draft Comprehensive Conservation Plan and Environment Assessment (Draft CCP/EA) for Logan Cave NWR was sought throughout the planning process. The planning team held one public scoping meeting and solicited public reaction to the proposed alternatives. Also, a 30-day public review and comment period of the Draft CCP/EA was provided.

The Service developed and analyzed three alternatives. Alternative 1 represented a custodial approach. Refuge management or resource protection would not occur; fish and wildlife populations would not be monitored, habitats would not be managed or monitored, no land protection would occur, and no law enforcement activities would be performed. Under this alternative, the Service would probably enter into management agreements with the Arkansas Game and Fish Commission and/or The Nature Conservancy.

Alternative 2 represented no change from current management of the refuge. All refuge management activities would have been directed toward achieving the refuge's primary purpose (to properly administer, conserve, and develop the 123-acre area for protection of a unique cave ecosystem that provides essential habitat for the endangered gray bat, endangered Benton cave crayfish, the threatened Ozark cavefish, and other significant cave dwelling wildlife species). Active habitat and wildlife management would continue to be limited to protection of the cave entrances and limited access to surface and subsurface habitats. Little to no environmental education and wildlife interpretation would occur. No improvements would be made to the exterior for wildlife observation or photography. Under this alternative, the refuge would not seek partnerships with adjacent landowners nor other state and federal agencies to contribute to the overall natural resource conservation effort in the area.

The primary focus under Alternative 3, the preferred alternative, will be to add a staff person and equipment in order to manage, maintain, restore, and protect the refuge's habitats and wildlife species. Intensive biological monitoring for all species of concern will occur. Active habitat management will be implemented to maintain and enhance water quantity and quality within the cave system, the recharge zone (ground water recharge areas), and waterways within the bat foraging areas through best management practices, easements, and partnerships with private landowners and other federal and state agencies. Continuous groundwater quality monitoring, which is crucial to the existence of the aquatic species utilizing the cave stream and groundwater corridors, will occur. Utilizing various partners, the refuge will develop a small environmental education program, focusing on karst environments. Limited staff- or volunteer-guided wildlife observation and photography and environmental education and interpretation will occur on the surface. The refuge will develop a community-based volunteer program by establishing a Cave Steward or Friends program.

The Service selected Alternative 3 as its preferred alternative and it is reflected in this CCP. Alternative 3 is selected for implementation because it properly administers, conserves, and develops the 123-acre area for protection of a unique cave ecosystem that provides essential habitat for the endangered gray bat, endangered Benton cave crayfish, the threatened Ozark cavefish, and other significant cave-dwelling wildlife species, while contributing to other national, regional and state goals to protect and restore karst habitats and species. At the same time, these management actions provide balanced levels of compatible public use opportunities consistent with existing laws, Service policies, and sound biological principles. It provides the best mix of program elements to achieve desired long-term conditions.

Under this alternative, all lands under the management and direction of the refuge will be protected, managed, maintained, and enhanced and those lands adjacent to the refuge will be prioritized for protection to best achieve national, regional, ecosystem, and refuge-specific goals and objectives within anticipated funding and staffing levels. In addition, the action positively addresses significant issues and concerns expressed by the public.

I. Background

INTRODUCTION

The U.S. Fish and Wildlife Service (Service) has developed this Comprehensive Conservation Plan (CCP) for Logan Cave National Wildlife Refuge (Logan Cave NWR) to guide management actions and direction for the refuge. Fish and wildlife conservation will receive first priority in refuge management; wildlife-dependent recreation will be allowed and encouraged as long as it is compatible with, and does not detract from, the mission of the refuge or the purposes for which it was established.

A planning team developed a range of alternatives that best met the goals and objectives of the refuge and that could be implemented within the 15-year plan period. This CCP describes the Service's preferred management action. The Draft Comprehensive Conservation Plan and Environmental Assessment (Draft CCP/EA) was made available to state and federal government agencies, conservation partners, and the general public for review and comment. Comments from each entity were considered in the development of this Final CCP.

PURPOSE AND NEED FOR THE PLAN

The purpose of the CCP is to develop an action that best achieves the refuge purpose; attains the vision and goals developed for the refuge; contributes to National Wildlife Refuge System mission; addresses key problems, issues and relevant mandates; and is consistent with sound principles of fish and wildlife management.

Specifically, the plan is needed to:

- Provide a clear statement of refuge management direction;
- Provide refuge neighbors, visitors, and government officials with an understanding of Service management actions on and around the refuge;
- Ensure that Service management actions, including land protection and recreation/education programs, are consistent with the mandates of the National Wildlife Refuge System;
- Ensure that refuge management is consistent with the purpose for which the refuge was established;
- Ensure that refuge management is consistent with federal, state, and local plans and contributes to the mission of the ecosystem it is located in; and
- Provide a basis for the development of budget requests for operations, maintenance, and capital improvement needs.

Perhaps the greatest need of the Service is communication with the public and the public's participation in carrying out the mission of the National Wildlife Refuge System. Many agencies, organizations, institutions, and businesses have developed relationships with the Service to advance the mission of national wildlife refuges.

FISH AND WILDLIFE SERVICE

As part of its mission, the Service manages more than 540 national wildlife refuges, covering over 95 million acres. These areas comprise the National Wildlife Refuge System, the world's largest collection of lands set aside specifically for fish and wildlife. The majority of these lands, 77 million acres, is in Alaska. The remaining acres are spread across the other 49 states and several United States territories. In addition to refuges, the Service manages thousands of small wetlands, national fish hatcheries, 64 fishery resource offices, and 78 ecological services field stations. The Service enforces federal wildlife laws, administers the Endangered Species Act, manages migratory bird populations, restores nationally significant fisheries, conserves and restores wildlife habitat, and helps foreign governments with their conservation efforts. It also oversees the Federal Aid program that distributes hundreds of millions of dollars in excise taxes on fishing and hunting equipment to state fish and wildlife agencies.

NATIONAL WILDLIFE REFUGE SYSTEM

The mission of the National Wildlife Refuge System, as defined by the National Wildlife Refuge System Improvement Act of 1997 is:

> "...to administer a national network of lands and waters for the conservation, management, and where appropriate, restoration of the fish, wildlife and plant resources and their habitats within the United States for the benefit of present and future generations of Americans."

NATIONAL WILDLIFE REFUGE SYSTEM IMPROVEMENT ACT OF 1997

An important milestone occurred in 1997 with the passage of the National Wildlife Refuge System Act (Improvement Act), which has been called the "Organic Act" of the Refuge System. The Improvement Act established, for the first time, a clear legislative mission of wildlife conservation for the National Wildlife Refuge System.

Actions were initiated in 1997 to comply with the direction of this new legislation, including an effort to CCPs for all refuges. These CCPs, which are completed with full public involvement, help guide the future management of refuges by establishing natural resources and recreation/education programs. Consistent with the Improvement Act, approved CCPs will serve as the guidelines for refuge management for the next 15 years. The Improvement Act states that each refuge shall be managed to:

- Fulfill the mission of the National Wildlife Refuge System;
- Fulfill the individual purposes of each refuge;
- Consider the needs of wildlife first;
- Fulfill requirements of comprehensive conservation plans that are prepared for each unit of the refuge system;
- Maintain the biological integrity, diversity, and environmental health of the refuge system; and
- Recognize that wildlife-dependent recreation activities including hunting, fishing, wildlife observation, wildlife photography, and environmental education and interpretation are legitimate and priority public uses; and allow refuge managers authority to determine compatible public uses.

The National Wildlife Refuge System (Refuge System) hosts over 38 million annual visitors. Economists found that these refuge visitors contribute more than $400 million annually to local economies. In 2001, on conservation lands throughout the nation, approximately 37.8 million people participated in wildlife-related activities, most to observe wildlife in their natural habitats. These visitors represented nearly 40 percent of the county's adults who spent $108 billion on wildlife-related pursuits in 2001, according to the National Survey of Fishing, Hunting and Wildlife Associated Recreation (U.S. Department of Interior, Fish and Wildlife Service and U.S. Department of Commerce, U. S. Census Bureau 2002). As visitation continues to grow on conservation lands and waters in general and specifically on refuges, adjacent local communities are realizing significant economic benefits.

Volunteers continue to be a major contributor to the success of the Refuge System. In 2002, volunteers contributed more than 1.5 million hours on refuges nationwide, a service valued at more than $22 million.

The wildlife and habitat vision for national wildlife refuges stresses that wildlife comes first; that ecosystems, biodiversity, and wilderness are vital concepts in refuge management; that refuges must be healthy and growth must be strategic; and that the Refuge System serves as a model for habitat management with broad participation from others.

LEGAL AND POLICY CONTEXT

Administration of national wildlife refuges is guided by the mission and goals of the Refuge System, congressional legislation, presidential executive orders, and international treaties. Policies for management options of refuges are further refined by administrative guidelines established by the Secretary of the Interior and by policy guidelines established by the Director of the Fish and Wildlife Service. Refer to Appendix C for a complete listing of relevant legal mandates.

Lands within the Refuge System are closed to public use unless specifically and legally opened. All programs and uses must be evaluated based on mandates set forth in the Improvement Act. Those mandates are to:

- Contribute to ecosystem goals, as well as refuge purposes and goals;
- Conserve, manage, and restore fish, wildlife, and plant resources and their habitats;
- Monitor the trends of fish, wildlife, and plants;
- Manage and ensure appropriate visitor uses as those uses benefit the conservation of fish and wildlife resources and contribute to the enjoyment of the public; and
- Ensure that visitor activities are compatible with refuge purposes.

The Improvement Act further identifies six priority wildlife-dependent recreational uses: hunting, fishing, wildlife observation, wildlife photography, and environmental education and interpretation. As priority public uses of the Refuge System, they receive priority consideration over other public uses in planning and management.

NATIONAL AND INTERNATIONAL CONSERVATION PLANS AND INITIATIVES

Multiple partnerships have been developed among government and private entities to address the environmental problems affecting regions. There is a large amount of conservation and protection information that defines the role of the refuge at the local, national, international, and ecosystem levels. Conservation initiatives include broad-scale planning and cooperation between affected parties to address declining trends of natural, physical, social, and economic environments. The conservation guidance described below, along with issues, problems, and trends, was reviewed and integrated where appropriate into this CCP.

This CCP supports the recovery plans for the gray bat, Indiana bat, Ozark cavefish (*Amblyopsis rosae*), Benton Cave crayfish (*Cambarus aculabrum*), and supports the Partners for Amphibians and Reptile Conservation (PARC) Plan.

Gray Bat Recovery Plan. This plan was completed in 1982 and provides priorities for protection and management of caves, guidelines for protection of foraging habitat, public education, and monitoring procedures. Logan Cave NWR was purchased mainly to protect the maternity gray bat colony that uses the cave.

Indiana Bat Recovery Plan. The original plan was approved in 1983 and revised in 2007 by the Indiana Bat Recovery Team. The plan provides the current status of the Indiana bat, its habitat requirements, and limiting factors and actions needed for recovery.

Ozark Cavefish (*Amblyopsis* rosae) Recovery Plan. This plan was completed in 1989 and outlines distribution, status, habitat requirements, limiting factors, and causes of decline for the Ozark cavefish. Several of the recovery actions listed in the plan have been implemented at Logan Cave NWR.

Recovery Plan for the Benton Cave Crayfish (*Cambarus aculabrum*). This species was listed as endangered in 1993 and the recovery plan was completed in 1996. At that time, *C. aculabrum* was known to exist in only two caves in northwest Arkansas, Logan Cave and Bear Hollow Cave. Since then, two additional populations were discovered although together they only represent a total of two crayfish. The plan outlines known habitat requirements, limiting factors, and actions needed for recovery.

Partners for Amphibians and Reptile Conservation (PARC) Plan. This plan was founded in 1998 to address the need for conservation of herpetofauna – amphibians and reptiles – and their habitats. Its mission is to conserve amphibians, reptiles, and their habitats as integral parts of the ecosystem and culture through proactive and coordinated public/private partnerships.

RELATIONSHIP TO STATE WILDLIFE AGENCY

A provision of the Improvement Act, and subsequent agency policy, is that the Service shall ensure timely and effective cooperation and collaboration with other state fish and game agencies and tribal governments during the course of acquiring and managing refuges. State wildlife management areas and national wildlife refuges provide the foundation for the protection of species, and contribute to the overall health and diversity of fish and wildlife species in the State of Arkansas.

The Arkansas Game and Fish Commission (AGFC) is a state-partnering agency with the Service, charged with enforcement responsibilities relating to migratory birds and endangered species, as well as managing state natural resources including over 100 lakes and wildlife management areas spanning thousands of acres. The AGFC has a perpetual goal to improve hunting and fishing opportunities for the sportsmen of the state, but it also realizes that a healthy environment for our fish and wildlife assures a healthy environment for the citizens of Arkansas. AGFC's participation and contribution throughout this planning process will provide for ongoing opportunities and open dialogue to improve the ecological diversity of fish and wildlife in Arkansas. A vital part of the comprehensive conservation planning process is integrating common mission objectives where appropriate.

II. Refuge Overview

INTRODUCTION AND PURPOSES

Logan Cave NWR covers 123 acres (50 hectares) near the northwest corner of Benton County, Arkansas (Figures 1 and 2), and includes a limestone solution cave with approximately 1.5 miles of passageways. The refuge was established in 1989 to protect cave inhabitants, including the endangered gray bat (*Myotis grisescens*), Benton cave crayfish (*Cambarus aculabrum*), and the threatened Ozark cavefish (*Amblyopsis rosae*). The cave also has historically provided habitat for the endangered Indiana bat (*Myotis sodalis*).

There are only two known entry points for the cave: the sinkhole and spring. The sinkhole consists of a steep sided funnel shaped depression about 50 feet in diameter located on a forested hillside. The spring entrance is located on a hillside under an overhang rock bluff. Most of the refuge consists of hillsides which support a mature climax community of oak and hickory.

Groundwater surfacing within the cave forms a stream which flows throughout the cave and at the outfall forms Logan Spring, which drains to Osage Creek just south of the refuge. Osage Creek is a major tributary of the Illinois River, which is the main drainage in southwestern Benton County, and their confluence is about 1.2 miles south of the refuge. In past years, spring water from the cave had a measured flow of approximately 5 million gallons per day and supplied the Logan community, a fish hatchery, and 49 fish ponds.

ECOSYSTEM CONTEXT

Logan Cave NWR is administratively located within an area designated by the Service as the Arkansas/Red Rivers Ecosystem (Ark/Red), which contains approximately 245,000 square miles and extends from the Rocky Mountains of Colorado to the bayous of Louisiana, and includes all of Oklahoma and parts of seven other states, including western parts of Arkansas (Figure 3). Elevations within the Ark/Red range from more than 14,000 feet ngvd (national geodetic vertical datum) to less than 300 feet ngvd along the Red River in Louisiana. Because of the diversity in land forms, soils, average annual precipitation, and other factors, the Ark/Red supports the greatest diversity of fish and wildlife and wildlife resources of any Service ecosystem nationwide.

There are 16 defined ecoregions that occur within the Ark/Red. One of those ecoregions is the Ozark Highlands. The Ozark Highlands (approximately 50,000 square miles) is in the states of Arkansas, Oklahoma, Missouri, and a small portion of Kansas. It is a dome-shaped uplift composed of four distinct areas (Boston Mountains, St. Francois Mountains, Salem Plateau, and Springfield Plateau). Logan Cave NWR is located within the Springfield Plateau of the Ozark Highlands Ecoregion.

The highest elevations reach above 1,500 feet ngvd, with the general slope of the area to the southwest, and drainage primarily to the Illinois and Neosho rivers. The natural communities of this ecoregion are dominated by a western extension of the oak-hickory forest. More mesic floodplain forests occur along the major streams of the region. Another dominant feature of the Ozarks Highlands is the extensive network of cave habitats formed in the underlying limestone bedrock. Numerous rare, endangered, and endemic fish and wildlife species are associated with and are dependent upon these habitats. The most critical resource issues in the Ark/Red center on management of water quality and quantity.

Figure 1. Vicinity map of Logan Cave NWR

Figure 2. Management boundary for Logan Cave NWR

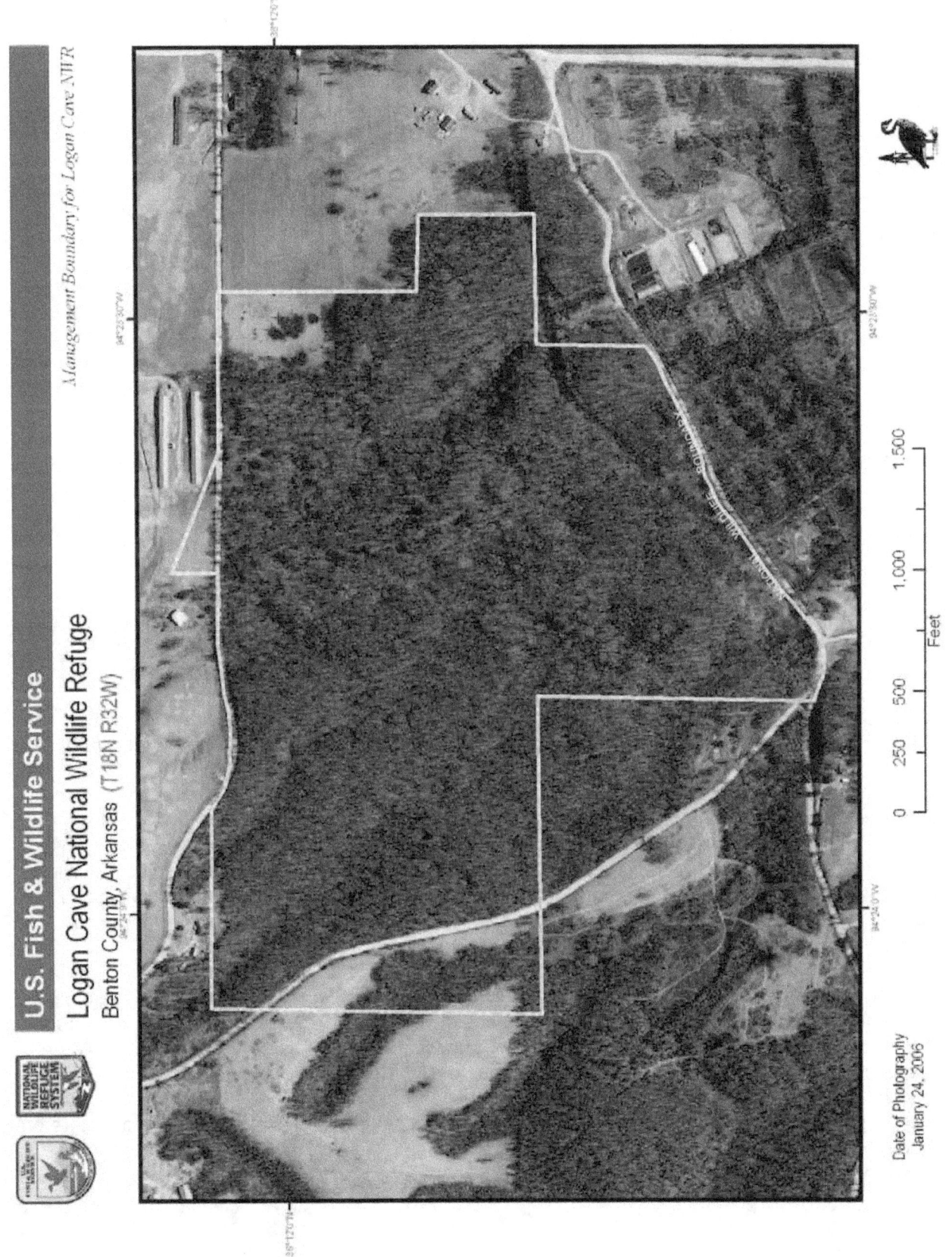

U.S. Fish & Wildlife Service

Logan Cave National Wildlife Refuge
Benton County, Arkansas (T18N R32W)

Management Boundary for Logan Cave NWR

Date of Photography
January 24, 2006

Because of its location, Logan Cave NWR has a close association with Bailey's classification of the Ozark Ecoregion and the Service's Ozark Ecosystem. Past and future participation with the Ozark Ecosystem has and will continue to increase coordination and conservation efforts.

ECOLOGICAL THREATS AND PROBLEMS

Factors most likely to limit or cause a decline in the species inhabiting Logan Cave NWR include the following: (1) destruction of habitat including water quality degradation; (2) disturbance by cavers or trespassers; (3) collecting; and (4) low reproductive potential of cave fauna.

1. Groundwater contamination problems are common in cave regions. Unfortunately, most of the public perceives that the subsurface cleanses wastewater and subsurface disposal of waste is practical and harmless. Most of the water which enters caves and spring systems, such as Logan Cave, do not receive effective natural cleansing. Thomas Aley of the Ozark Underground laboratory mapped the recharge areas for Logan Spring in 1987, and delineated the areas into the following categories:

    A) <u>Low Hazard Areas</u>: These are lands located near, yet apparently outside of the Logan Spring recharge areas.

    B) <u>Moderate Hazard Areas</u>: These are lands which are topographically tributary to the Logan Spring recharge area. Groundwater directly beneath these areas does not appear to routinely discharge through Logan Spring. Under moderate- and high-flow conditions, some waters from these areas will enter the groundwater systems and discharge through Logan Spring.

    C) <u>High Hazard Areas</u>: These are lands which are known or presumed to lie within the groundwater recharge area for Logan Spring. High Hazard Areas exclude losing stream valleys and areas which contribute groundwater solely to Logan Spring.

    D) <u>Extremely High Hazard Areas</u>: These are losing stream valleys in the Logan Spring recharge area, or, they are lands which contribute groundwater solely to Logan Spring.

According to Aley, two major classes of land-use activities occur in the Logan Cave recharge zones and surrounding areas: residential/light commercial development and agriculture. If runoff of high concentrations of harmful biological (i.e., fecal Coliform, E. coli) or chemical (i.e., pesticides) pollutants occur, or high concentrations of nitrates and phosphates are present, a biological oxygen demand (BOD) and chemical oxygen demand (COD) can occur and place an abnormal oxygen demand on the aquatic cave, spring, and river fauna. The following are some potential impacts of land use activities in the recharge areas of Logan Spring:

<u>Agriculture and waste disposal activities</u>: Numerous farms with cattle, hogs, and poultry operate within the recharge areas of Logan Cave and produce substantial quantities of animal waste. Large quantities of animal waste entering groundwater will deplete dissolved oxygen in subsurface water and can severely impact aquatic cave fauna. Adequate treatment of animal wastes is typically expensive and often not attempted. There is no incentive from local or federal government agencies to encourage adequate and careful disposal of large quantities of animal waste in Arkansas, therefore the cheapest and easiest disposal method is utilized: land application. The waste does serve as fertilizer and can enhance grass production in most areas. The farmers are usually left to apply the

waste as often as they feel necessary and unfortunately without much regard to runoff effects. In karst areas like Logan Cave, waste can significantly impact groundwater quality if it rapidly enters groundwater systems, especially after rainfall sufficient to cause overland runoff following a recent land application of animal waste.

Residential and commercial land development: Since the construction and operation of the Northwest Regional Airport at Highfill, Arkansas, land values in the vicinity of the cave have increased substantially, with a great deal of real estate development and road construction in the areas surrounding Logan Cave NWR. With the residential development boom, commercial development will inevitably follow. Leaks and spills of hazardous materials occur frequently from roads and commercial businesses. A substantial amount of the groundwater contamination from residential and commercial development occurs from inadequate sewage disposal systems. Septic field systems routinely use on-lot disposal in most of northwest Arkansas' karst region which produces groundwater contamination and pollution. The potential of this impending groundwater contamination is sufficient to endanger cave fauna.

Increasing utilization of the water in the cave poses a threat to the aquatic habitat and the cave's aquatic species. A past attempt to drill into the reservoir of water in the cave was unsuccessful. The shaft entered the cave but missed the water, despite surveying by a geologist to direct the drilling. Current and future surveying techniques would make drilling directly into the cave stream possible. Water is currently being pumped from the pool, which is formed by the spring to supply a large poultry operation, several residences, and a plant/tree nursery. During periods of drought, the water pumped from the spring could affect water levels within the cave stream, which would obviously have a negative impact on the cave's aquatic habitat and species.

Transportation and pipeline routes: Construction and maintenance of roads and pipelines can cause sediments to enter into groundwater systems. This problem can be avoided through the use of good current methods to reduce surface soil erosion. Leaks and spills that could occur in the recharge area for Logan Cave NWR's groundwater system could have a serious effect on the water quality and cave fauna.

Loss of foraging habitat for the gray bat: Development within the recharge area of the cave and along the Osage River and surrounding woodlands is decreasing the foraging area for Logan Cave NWR's gray bat maternity colony. In 1968, 59 percent of the recharge area was forested; this had decreased to 43 percent by 1987, and has steadily decreased until the only forested areas are along creek bottoms or ridge tops where it is too steep for livestock or poultry operations. Adult gray bats feed on insects almost exclusively over water and in forest canopies along river or reservoir edges. Also, whenever possible, gray bats of all ages fly in the protection of forest canopy between caves and feeding areas for increased protection from predators such as screech owls. Construction of houses, paving of roads, and clearing of forests impose a risk of lower water quality for this karst area. Insects that the bats feed on are quite sensitive to aquatic pollution. Logan Cave NWR's gray bat maternity colony may decrease as the forest canopy declines and development, with the inevitable chemical pollution and siltation of the waterways over which the gray bats forage, increases.

2. Trespass has decreased greatly since both entrances were fenced and gated. But, despite protection afforded the cave, trespass in the cave will continue to be a problem. Disturbance by people entering the cave impacts the physical conditions for individual cavefish and crayfish. Obligate cave dwellers have a low metabolic level and have limited opportunities to feed and reproduce, therefore physical activity that results from disturbances uses up energy that the cavefish and crayfish need in feeding and reproducing. Physical disturbance is a direct threat because it agitates stream bottom sediments, causing turbidity and reducing visibility, which greatly increases the likelihood that a crayfish or cavefish may be stepped on, causing injury or mortality. Disturbances

can interrupt breeding or feeding activities of the crayfish, cavefish, and gray bat, along with other cave species. It is especially important to protect the maternity colony of gray bats at Logan Cave NWR because both the crayfish and cavefish rely indirectly or directly on the bat guano (organic input) for food. Disturbance inside the cave or near the cave entrances could result in bat mortality, abandonment of the cave, and the loss of an energy source for both the crayfish and cavefish.

3. Most troglobitic (cave adapted) species have a low reproductive rate and need a relatively long period to reach maturity. Removal of any cave crayfish or cavefish by collectors will affect the ability of the species to reproduce. Loss of mature individuals capable of reproducing obviously causes a decline in population levels.

4. Although the cave entrances are owned by the Service and are protected, most of the recharge zone for Logan Cave, Logan Spring, and foraging areas for the bats is privately owned. Past water quality studies by the University of Arkansas at Fayetteville have shown that the Logan Cave stream has good water quality, with the exception of high fecal coliform counts in the summer. This indicates heavy agricultural use of the watershed that should be monitored carefully along with dissolved oxygen that could also be affected by agricultural and residential material.

Maintaining the aquatic and terrestrial ecosystems at Logan Cave NWR will require more than preventing trespass into the cave and protection of the recharge zones. It will require educating adjacent landowners and others about the sensitivity of karst systems, and it will take an ecosystem approach to protecting the variety of resources dependent on northwest Arkansas' karst topography through partnerships with private landowners, conservation and caving organizations, universities, and state and federal conservation agencies. With the help of these partners, management agreements can be developed with private landowners, and easements and lands can be purchased from willing sellers.

PHYSICAL RESOURCES

CLIMATE

Because of its geographic location, northwest Arkansas' weather is characterized by sudden and dramatic changes in temperature and climate as warm moist air from the Gulf of Mexico battles it out with cold air from Canada and hot dry air from the southwest. The average high temperature is 68 degrees Fahrenheit and the average low is 44 degrees Fahrenheit. The recorded high and low temperatures are 114 degrees Fahrenheit and -15 degrees Fahrenheit, respectively. Average rainfall is 45 inches and the average snowfall is 12 inches. The first frost of the cold season typically occurs between October 9 and October 13, and the last frost of the season typically occurs between April 8 and April 19.

GEOLOGY AND TOPOGRAPHY

Logan Cave NWR is located in the NW ¼ NE ¼ Section 33, T18N, R32W, Benton County, Arkansas. The elevation of Logan Spring (lower entrance) is 1,040 feet and the sinkhole entrance is at 1,100 feet. This area is typical of the Ozarks with rocky soils, numerous caves, losing streams, springs and underground rivers. The landscape around Logan Cave NWR is picturesque with gently rolling hills, springs, streams, pasture, and wooded hillsides giving way to the Osage Creek valley.

Geographically, Logan Cave NWR is located within the Springfield Plateau geologic province on the southwest flank of the Ozark Dome, which is a broad uplift centered in southeast Missouri. The Springfield Plateau is comprised of bedrock units formed from sediments deposited by

Paleozoic seas. These bedrock units dip gently to the south, and many are cut by normal faults with downward motion on their south sides. The upper part of the Springfield Plateau is composed of cherty limestone of the Lower Mississippian Boone Formation, which is underlain by chert-free limestone of the St. Joe Formation.

Logan Cave NWR is underlain by generally flat-lying bedrock of the St. Joe Formation. Springs often discharge from caves and conduits in the St. Joe Formation due to the impermeable nature of the underlying Chattanooga Shale. Chattanooga Shale underlies the refuge at shallow depths. The shale is exposed to the south because elevations in the area decrease to the south. A normal fault is mapped along the east boundary of the refuge. The regional water table, which occurs in the St. Joe-Boone aquifer, has been mapped at a depth of 75 feet in the vicinity of the sinkhole entrance to Logan Cave. It seems that Logan Cave may have formed because groundwater perched on chert beds or low-permeability limestone beds flowed preferentially through fractures formed by tectonic activity on the nearby fault, resulting in dissolution of surrounding limestone.

SOILS

According to the Soil Survey of Benton County, Arkansas, Clarksville series soils cover the majority of the hill slopes near Logan Cave, whereas Nixa series soils cover the ridge tops. Clarksville soils form from very cherty limestone and generally consist of a cherty silt loam with high permeability and moderate strength. These soils typically are classified in accordance with the Unified Soil Classification System as silty, clayey, or poorly graded gravel. The fine-grained fraction of Clarksville soils is non-plastic to slightly plastic and has low potential for swelling and shrinking with variations in moisture content. Nixa series soils are very similar to Clarksville soils, except that the Nixa soils have very low permeability. Both soil series generally are brown to yellowish brown, although the Nixa soils grade to reddish brown near bedrock. Both soil series grade into weathered bedrock and fill fractures within the upper parts of the bedrock.

HYDROLOGY

The Boone and St. Joe Formations form the dominant groundwater aquifer in northwestern Arkansas. Chert content within the Boone Formation ranges from a few to 70 percent, and laterally extensive chert layers have been observed to perch groundwater at different zones within the formation. Overall, groundwater within the Boone-St. Joe aquifer is perched upon the underlying Chattanooga Shale. Both the Boone and St. Joe formations are dissected by numerous caves and solution channels. Groundwater flow within the Boone-St. Joe aquifer occurs preferentially through solution channels, including caves, fault zones, and fractures. The widespread occurrence of solution channels also affects surface water, resulting in disappearing streams and springs throughout the area. More than 90 percent of springs in northwest Arkansas with discharge in excess of 3.4 million gallons per day are within 1,600 feet of faults, and many fault zones and fault-related fractures have associated parallel caves and solution channels that formed by preferential groundwater flow.

The recharge zone for Logan Cave is described by Aley and Aley (1987) as 3,015 hectares (7,450 acres) in area lying north and east of the cave entrance. The recharge zone is the surface and groundwater regions that contribute water to the Logan Cave stream and spring. Nearly the entire recharge zone for Logan Cave is underlain by the St. Joe Formation. The surface streams are primarily discrete losing streams that flow through mostly agricultural land. In 1968, 59 percent of the recharge zone was forested; this had decreased to 43 percent by 1987 and has steadily decreased until the only forested areas are along creek bottoms or ridge tops where it is too steep for livestock or poultry operations.

AIR QUALITY

Benton County ranks high in the state and the nation for smog and air borne pollutants and is at the top of the list of Arkansas counties for pollutants due to animal waste (primarily poultry). Air quality in the area of the refuge is good because of its mostly rural nature. Local industries and urban concentrations of vehicles lessen the overall air quality of the county.

WATER QUALITY AND QUANITY

Caves, their recharge zones, and surrounding habitats are extremely important to certain species. The flora and fauna in and around caves serves as an indicator of the Ozark's environmental quality because it suffers from a number of the same factors affecting the human environment. Groundwater quality is vital to the health of most cave dwellers, as well as to the region's people who rely on wells for water. Such is the case with Logan Cave.

During the 1990s, water quality was tested in Logan Cave and compared with water quality of surface streams within the recharge area. Water quality measurements for the cave system were strongly correlated with water quality of the surface streams. All water quality sample parameters showed no significant difference between surface and cave streams. Water quality for Logan Cave and the recharge streams were well below the U.S. Environmental Protection Agency (EPA) limits for environmental compounds except for fecal coliform. Fecal coliform counts were always above the EPA drinking water standards. Similar comparisons between Logan Cave and recharge streams were noted for conductivity, phosphorus, and total phosphorus. Alkalinity for Logan Cave was comparable to the other highland streams. Water samples tested for heavy metals and pesticides fell within the domestic water supply standards set forth by the EPA.

BIOLOGICAL RESOURCES

HABITAT

The Logan Cave area has a very diverse habitat which includes representatives of several Ozark Mountain types: oak-hickory forest, grassland, shrubland, floodplain, marshland, bottomland hardwood, upland deciduous, and a small prairie. The cave entrances provide particularly rich habitat and consist of extensive rock overhangs with subdued lighting that maintains a higher humidity than the surrounding oak-hickory forest. The resulting environment supports a variety of plant and animal life forms.

A spring-fed stream, with an average water flow of 5 million gallons per day, extends the entire length of the cave. This stream, fed by small springs that emanate from the cave, flows into a natural oxbow lake and then into the Osage Creek, a large tributary of the Illinois River.

The northwestern third of the refuge consists of hillsides which support a mature climax community of oak and hickory. The climax forest growing on the slopes surrounding the cave's sinkhole entrance provides natural organic litter to the cave ecosystem for a food energy base. Leaves that fall through the sinkhole and into the stream are the base energy source for the cave's aquatic fauna. Upstream from the sinkhole, the cave area contains several large seeps which cascade down the walls from the ceiling. These seeps introduce organic matter in the form of fine particulates and dissolved material. These organic materials supply nutrients for many inhabitants of the cave.

Logan Cave is a large limestone-solution cave with approximately 1.5 miles of surveyed passageways. The three ecological classification types (tunnel, seepage, and sinkhole) are present in different sections of the cave. The sinkhole and spring entrances are the only two known entry points. The sinkhole consists of a funnel-shaped depression about 50 feet in diameter on a forested hillside. The spring entrance is located on a hillside under an overhang rock bluff. The cave's passageway is relatively narrow with a low ceiling. In some areas, the ceiling gradually declines, leaving only a tiny crawl space. Approximately halfway through the cave is an area with a high dome ceiling where gray bats congregate their maternity colony.

For past research projects and descriptive purposes, the cave was divided into three reaches, separated conveniently by morphological features. The lower reach is 365 m long and includes the distance from the mouth of the cave (spring) to the sinkhole. This section is typified by shallow (10 to 20 cm) riffles with only a single 10 m long pool (approximately 1 m deep) near the mouth of the cave. The middle reach is 220 m in length and consists of one continuous pool located upstream of the sinkhole. The pool attains a maximum depth of 2.5 m with a mean depth of approximately 1 m. The third reach extends upstream from the pool 685 m to a large ceiling collapse that limits further upstream access. The cave's internal temperature is a constant 55 degrees Fahrenheit.

WILDLIFE

Logan Cave's unique ecosystem provides essential habitat for the endangered gray bat (*Myotis grisescens*), endangered Benton Cave crayfish (*Cambarus aculabrum*), the threatened Ozark cavefish (*Amblyopsis rosae*), and historically the endangered Indiana bat (*Myotis sodalis*).

Adult female gray bats utilize the cave from March through August as a maternity site for raising their young. Each adult female will give birth to a single young in late May or early June. Most young begin to fly within 20-25 days after birth. Late summer emergent counts for Logan Cave average around 20,000. The 2005 summer survey yielded 30,000 bats, however, the summer surveys for 2006 and 2007 yielded only 5,170 and 11,530, respectively. The gray bat is probably one of the most restricted to cave habitats of any U.S. mammal. With rare exception, it roosts in caves year-round. Because of highly specific roost and habitat requirements, fewer that 5 percent of available caves are suitable for occupation by gray bats.

In the recovery plan for the Indiana bat, Benton County is historically noted for having Priority Three hibernacula (< 500 bats). Logan Cave was utilized in the past as hibernacula.

Logan Cave is one of only four known habitats for *Cambarus aculabrum*. Cave crayfish are highly specialized for living in stable cave environments with low light and low temperatures and are unable to cope with changes in their habitats that may be induced by human activities.

The threatened Ozark cavefish is found in 35 caves and springs in northwest Arkansas, southwest Missouri, and northeast Oklahoma. Logan Cave's population is the second largest known. All of the caves with cavefish contain some comparatively large source of allochthonous energy, usually bat guano and/or leaf litter.

Other interesting life forms found throughout the cave include: pseudoscorpions, isopods, amphipods, beetles, collembolans, and other insects which are blind, without pigment, and strictly adapted to a subterranean habitat. Additionally, the site is known to support at least two species of state conservation concern: grotto salamander (*Eurycea spelaeus*), and a cave obligate millipede (*Trigenotyla parca*).

The oak-hickory forest outside the cave provides homes for a variety of wildlife. The most visible mammalian species are squirrels, woodchucks, armadillos, skunks, and white-tailed deer. Several avian, amphibian, and reptilian species can be found around the refuge. Vultures, herons, swallows and hawks are the most visible birds. Amphibians and reptiles that can be observed on the refuge include: bullfrogs, green frogs, skinks, snapping turtles, and grotto salamanders. Other species that are abundant in the area include northern fence lizard, midland water snake, chorus tree frog, and the Ozark redback salamander.

CULTURAL RESOURCES

There has never been an archaeological investigation within the refuge by the Service. There is evidence of an old home place close to the mouth of the cave, and in the 1940s a cannery operated close to the mouth of the cave using the water from the spring. The remnants of an old fish hatchery remain just south of the refuge boundary and the old fish ponds were across the road. Water from the cave (Logan Spring) supplied the hatchery, fish ponds and the Logan community. Today, water from the spring supplies water for a large poultry operation, several residences, and a tree/plant nursery.

SOCIOECONOMIC ENVIRONMENT

Logan Cave NWR lies in the northwest corner of Benton County. Benton County is located in the northwest corner of Arkansas and adjoins Oklahoma to the west and Missouri to the north. The county seat is Bentonville, in the center of the county. Benton County was the first county established in the State of Arkansas in 1836.

Northwest Arkansas is one of the fastest growing areas in the nation and Benton County is the fastest growing county in the state. The related development is moving toward regions like the refuge that retain a rural atmosphere, yet remain close to cities that are bustling with economic activity.

Population change can be an indication of economic vitality, the types of economic sectors that are likely to be strong, probable development and disturbance impacts on wildlife habitat. The U.S. Census Bureau ranks Benton County 2nd in the state for total population. First is Pulaski County with the capital city of Little Rock. In April 2000, Benton County had a population of 153,406 and 179,756 in July 2006. That's a 27.8 percent increase (the highest in the state). The population percent change from 1990 to 2000 was 57.3 percent.

Poultry and cattle agribusiness, light manufacturing, retail distribution, retail support, and transportation are the most important economic sectors. Important agricultural crops include hay and pasture for livestock. Benton County leads the state and is third in the nation for broiler (poultry) production. Much of the Tyson's Foods' operation is located in Benton County and headquartered in adjacent Washington County.

There are several large manufacturing industries in Benton County, including Glad Manufacturing (Glad plastic bags and cling wrap), Kraft Foods (bulk cheese), Rogers Tool Works (carbide compacts for the oil industry and other drills and tools), Allen Canning (one of the country's top vegetable canning companies), Daisy Outdoor Products (the world's oldest and largest producer of airguns, BB guns, pellet rifles, and CO2 pistols), and J.B. Hunt (one of the nations largest trucking companies).

The world's largest company, Wal-Mart Stores, Inc., and its subsidiaries are headquartered in Bentonville. Numerous Fortune 500 companies (as well as smaller firms) have regional offices in Benton County to support their accounts at Wal-Mart. The newly constructed Northwest Arkansas Regional Airport is centrally located in Highfill; which is only a few miles from the refuge.

With major industries located nearby and the rapidly increasing population, development in the region has skyrocketed in the past few years. Real estate values have increased significantly and the once wooded landscape surrounding the refuge is quickly turning into houses, apartments, golf courses, and other commercial developments. The refuge is rapidly becoming a small island in a sea of development.

REFUGE ADMINISTRATION AND MANAGEMENT

LAND PROTECTION AND CONSERVATION

To protect the cave from trespassers and vandalism, the entire refuge, not just the cave, is closed to all public use. Both cave entrances have protection from trespass. The mouth of the cave or the spring entrance has a gate located up inside the cave. This was the only feasible way to protect the spring entrance and gray bats prefer internal gates. The sinkhole entrance was fenced with a steel fence that completely circles the entire sinkhole area.

To protect Logan Cave NWR for future generations, it will be necessary for the Service to continue protecting the cave, spring, and recharge zone; improve public understanding of Logan Cave's valuable resources; and develop and maintain public and private partnerships to protect not only the refuge but additional resources that are vulnerable to northwest Arkansas' rapid development.

VISITOR SERVICES

Due to the sensitive nature of the refuge's flora and fauna, public use, educational programs, and scientific research is limited. No one is allowed inside the cave from March through September to protect the gray bat maternity colony. Disturbance inside the cave before young are able to fly would cause the young to fall to their deaths as their frightened mothers hurried out of the cave. Also, walking through the cave increases turbidity with the potential to step on cavefish and crayfish.

PERSONNEL, OPERATIONS AND MAINTENANCE

Logan Cave NWR has never received any funding or been staffed. All operations and maintenance are provided through Holla Bend NWR. Site visits to the refuge seldom occur due to lack of staff and distance from Holla Bend NWR (160 miles, one way). Visits to the cave generally are for wildlife surveys and maintenance to signs, gates, and fences. The refuge relies to a great extent on karst biologists with The Nature Conservancy office in northwest Arkansas and karst biologists from the Service's Ecological Services office to keep refuge staff up-to-date on environmental activities and issues in the Logan Cave region.

Figure 3. Fish and Wildlife Service Ark/Red Rivers Ecosystem

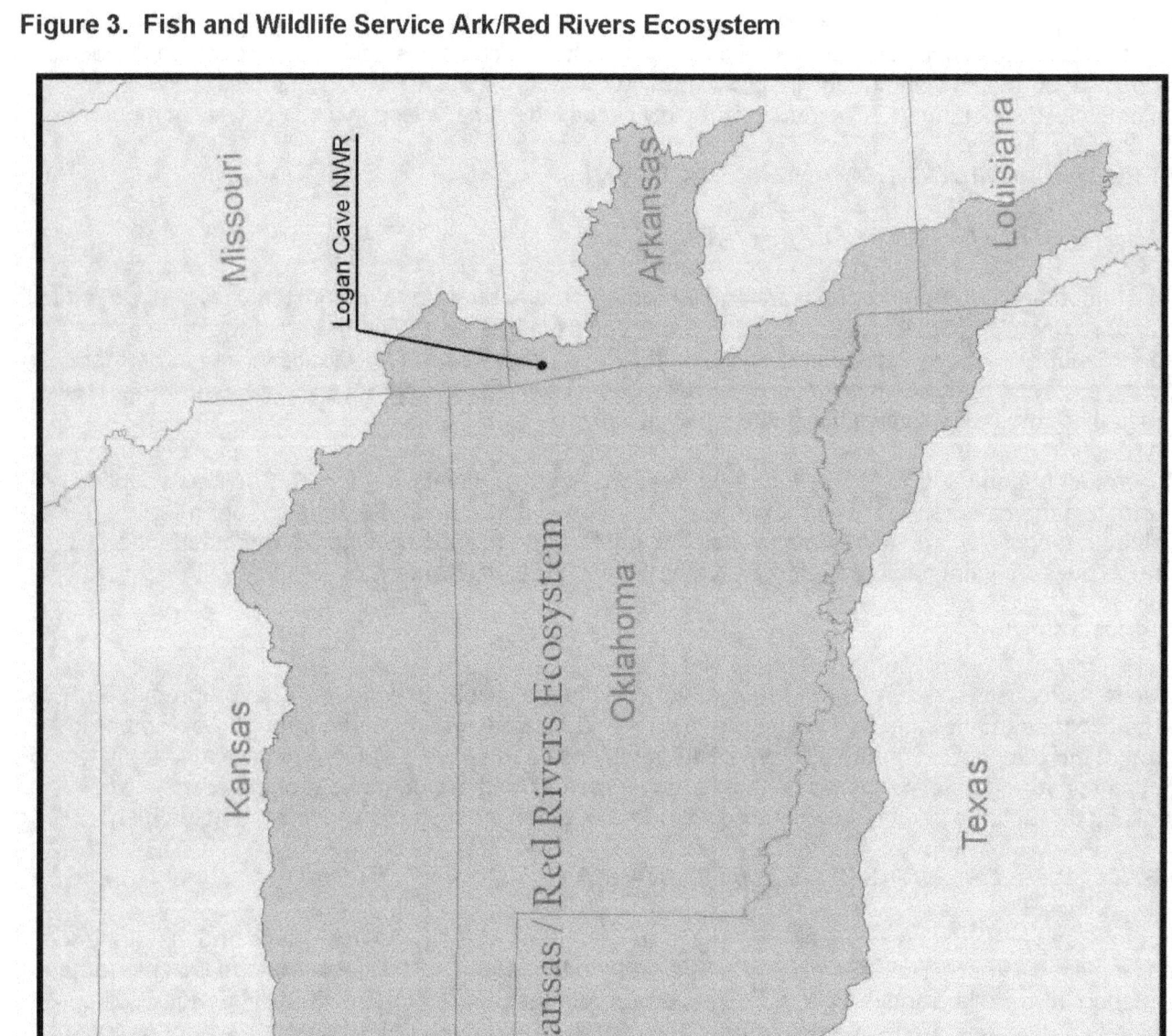

III. Plan Development

OVERVIEW

Early in the process of developing the Draft CCP/EA, the planning team identified a list of issues and concerns that were likely to be associated with the conservation and management of Logan Cave NWR.

PUBLIC INVOLVEMENT AND THE PLANNING PROCESS

In accordance with Service guidelines and National Environmental Policy Act recommendations, public involvement has been a crucial factor throughout the development of the CCP for Logan Cave NWR. This CCP has been written with input and assistance from interested citizens, conservation organizations, and employees of local and state agencies. The participation of these stakeholders and their ideas has been of great value in setting the management direction for the refuge. The Service, as a whole, and the refuge staff, in particular, are very grateful to each one who has contributed time, expertise, and ideas to the planning process. The staff remains impressed by the passion and commitment of so many individuals for the lands and waters administered by the refuge.

Initial CCP planning meetings were attended by refuge personnel. At these meetings, strategies for completing the CCP were discussed, issues and concerns were identified, and a mailing list of likely interested organizations and individuals was compiled. A planning team consisting of Service personnel from Arkansas and Oklahoma, representatives from The Nature Conservancy of Arkansas, and the Arkansas Game and Fish Commission were assembled where team members were introduced to the refuge and its planning process and asked to identify their issues and concerns. A public meeting was held in April 2006 for the same purposes as the scoping meeting. Announcements giving the location, date, and time for the public meeting were sent to local newspapers. The planning team met again after the public meeting to review individual goals and objectives and identify strategies and projects for this CCP.

SUMMARY OF ISSUES, CONCERNS AND OPPORTUNITIES

The planning team identified a number of issues, concerns, and opportunities related to fish and wildlife protection, habitat restoration, water quality, recreation, and management of threatened and endangered species. Additionally, the planning team considered federal and state mandates, as well as applicable local ordinances, regulations, and plans. The team also directed the process of obtaining public input through public scoping meetings, open planning team meetings, comment packets, and personal contacts. All public and advisory team comments were considered, however, some issues important to the public fall outside the scope of the decision to be made within this planning process. The team considered all issues that arose as a result of this planning process, and developed this CCP that attempts to balance the competing opinions regarding important issues. The team identified those issues that, in the team's best professional judgment, are most significant to the refuge. A summary of the significant issues follows.

FISH AND WILDLIFE POPULATION MANAGEMENT

THREATENED AND ENDANGERED SPECIES

Recovery and protection of threatened and endangered plants and animals is an important responsibility delegated to the Service and its national wildlife refuges. Furthermore, Logan Cave NWR was established in 1989 to conserve fish or wildlife which is listed as threatened or endangered. Four threatened or endangered animals use, or could use, Logan Cave NWR: endangered Benton cave crayfish (*Cambarus aculabrum*), endangered gray bat (*Myotis grisescens*), threatened Ozark cavefish (*Amblyopsis rosae*), and the endangered Indiana bat (*Myotis sodalis*).

Logan Cave is one of three caves and one spring in Benton County, Arkansas, where a known population of cave crayfish exists. Logan Cave supports the largest population of *Cambarus aculabrum* in Arkansas and the world. Logan Cave stream flows through the entire length of the cave, and provides habitat for the crayfish. Population numbers seem to be stable, but are generally low. The last survey was completed in 2006 with biologists observing 31 crayfish. Factors most likely to limit or cause the decline of the Benton cave crayfish are: (1) destruction of habitat including water quality degradation; (2) disturbance by trespassers; (3) collecting; (4) low reproductive rate; and (5) competition and predation by troglophilic species.

Logan Cave is one of 35 caves known to have a population of the Ozark cavefish; however, Logan Cave has the 2nd largest population in Arkansas, and throughout its range. The last survey was completed in 2006 with biologists observing 43 cavefish. Factors most likely to limit or cause the decline of the Ozark cavefish are: (1) habitat destruction; (2) collecting; (3) disturbance by trespassers; and (4) low reproductive rate.

The range of the gray bat is concentrated in the cave regions of Arkansas, Missouri, Kentucky, Tennessee, and Alabama. Gray bats are cave residents year-round, however, occupy different caves in summer and winter. Logan Cave is utilized as a maternity site by approximately ten to fifteen thousand female gray bats. Typically, the bats arrive in February/March and leave in September/October. This maternity colony utilizes a domed room between the sinkhole and spring entrance. Disturbance of the bats is a major concern especially when newborn young are present. Disturbance can result in the young dropping to their deaths from the cave's ceiling or being abandoned by their mother.

The range of the Indiana bat is in the eastern United States from Oklahoma, Iowa, and Wisconsin east to Vermont and south to northwestern Florida (Harvey 2000). The present total population is estimated at 457,374 with more than 67 percent hibernating at only nine locations in Missouri, Indiana, and Kentucky. Due to the habitat and internal environment, Logan Cave could be used by Indiana bats as a hibernacula. The bats hibernate from October to April, depending on climatic conditions. Hibernating bats form large, tight, compact clusters normally estimated at 300 – 400 bats per square foot. Approximately 2,500 Indiana bats are known to hibernate in 10 Arkansas caves.

KARST DEPENDANT SPECIES

As well as *A. rosae* and *C. aculabrum*, Logan Cave harbors several other aquatic troglobites. These include an isopod (*Caecidotea antricola*) and an amphipod (*Stygobromus ozarkensis*), and other insects which are blind, without pigment, and strictly adapted to a subterranean habitat. Troglophiles that inhabit the cave include the grotto salamander (*Eurycea spelaeus*), cave salamander (*Eurycea lucifuga*), and dark-sided salamander (*Eurycea longicauda melanopleura*). Banded sculpin (*Cottus carolinae*) and epigeal ringed crayfish (*Orconectes neglectus*) also enter the cave and live in light and dark zones.

NEOTROPICAL MIGRATORY BIRDS

Neotropical migratory birds are a species group of special management concern. Based on compiled lists of birds, approximately 75 species potentially use the surface habitat on Logan Cave NWR. Although this small refuge cannot provide ideal habitat for forest dwelling birds, potential management strategies need to be considered as part of this CCP.

HABITAT MANAGEMENT

LOGAN CAVE

Logan Cave is a large limestone-solution cave approximately 1.5 miles in length. The three ecological classification types (e.g., tunnel, seepage, and sinkhole) are present in different sections of the cave. The cave's internal temperature is 55 degrees Fahrenheit. The terrestrial cave environment is extremely stable and such stability is of primary importance to troglobitic organisms that inhabit the cave. However, the aquatic cave environment is not as stable due to the relationship with surface water entering the cave through the recharge zone.

The sinkhole and spring entrances are the only two known entry points. The sinkhole consists of a funnel shaped depression about 50 feet in diameter on a forested hillside and the spring entrance is located on a hillside under an overhanging rock bluff. Upstream from the sinkhole, the cave contains several large seeps which cascade down the walls from the ceiling. These seeps introduce organic matter in the form of fine particulates and dissolved material. These organic materials supply nutrients for many inhabitants of the cave.

The cave's passageway is relatively narrow with a low ceiling. In some areas, the ceiling gradually declines leaving only a tiny crawl space. Deep within the interior of the cave there are several waterfalls that cascade down the walls. Approximately halfway through the cave is an area where gray bats congregate their maternity colony. This room formed many years ago when large rock plates caved-in.

LOGAN STREAM

Logan Stream extends the entire length of the cave and emerges at the mouth as Logan Spring, which has an average water flow of approximately 5 million gallons per day. The spring flows into a natural oxbow lake and then into Osage Creek, a major tributary of the Illinois River. Water clarity in Logan Stream is very high, except after storm events that result in increased flow and decreased clarity. Water quality is high except for seasonal increases in coliform bacteria associated with livestock operations in the recharge zone and traces of pharmaceuticals and other organic wastewater constituents from inadequate septic systems. To ensure success of all species in Logan Cave, water quality needs to remain at a constant high level.

As described by Means 1995, Logan Stream is divided into three reaches classified by habitat types. The lowermost reach is 365 m long and extends from the cave mouth upstream to the sinkhole. This reach consists of runs and riffles, with the substrate being primarily rock and rubble. The middle reach consists of a 230 m long pool that extends from the sinkhole to the next upstream riffle. Rock and silt comprised most of the substrate, with the maximum depth being 3 m. The third reach is 685 m and extends upstream from the pool to point where the cave roof meets the stream. This reach includes pools, riffles, and runs, with gravel, silt, and bedrock substrates.

SURFACE HABITAT

The surface of Logan Cave NWR is a diverse mix of habitats which include representatives of several Ozark Mountain types: oak-hickory forest, grassland, shrubland, bottomland hardwood, and upland deciduous. The refuge was established for the species which utilize the cave, however, the 123 acres of surface habitat and potential management techniques need to be addressed in this CCP.

LAND PROTECTION

RECHARGE ZONE

The recharge zone is described by Aley and Aley (1987) as 3,015 hectares (7,450 acres) in area, lying north and east of the cave entrance (Figure 4). The surface streams in the recharge zone are primarily discrete sinking streams that flow through mostly agricultural pasture land. Two major classes of land-use occur in the recharge zone: (1) residential/commercial use, and (2) agriculture. The recharge zone has numerous livestock operations, including approximately 50 hog and poultry houses from which Aley and Aley (1987) identified three potential types of impacts. First, feedlots and animal houses are normally on well-drained slopes which lead to runoff during heavy rains. These runoff waters may contain high levels of biological or chemical pollutants which can have a negative impact on Logan Stream. Second, farmers will occasionally dispose of wastes on unused areas of their property. These areas may be located in areas where runoff could reach stream sources and eventually Logan Stream. Third, toxins and chemicals in animal feeds can pass through the animals and reach streams, via land application of wastes. Aley and Aley (1987) stated that two major impacts of residential/commercial development are inappropriate sewage disposal and increased erosion or storm runoff. Recovery of the species utilizing Logan Cave is directly related to the water quality in Logan Stream, which is directly affected by land uses within the recharge zone.

Aley delineated the recharge zone into hazard areas to identify those surface areas which have differing potentials for the introduction of groundwater contaminants into Logan Cave: (1) low hazard; (2) moderate hazard; (3) high hazard; and (4) very high hazard areas; the higher the hazard, the higher in *priority* for protection of these areas. Based on these delineations this CCP will address strategies to protect these areas. Management techniques include conservation easements, fee title acquisition, nutrient management plans, and best management practices for landowners in the recharge zone.

BAT FORAGING AREA

Summer caves, especially those used by maternity colonies, are nearly always located within a kilometer of rivers or reservoirs over which the bats feed. Adult gray bats feed almost exclusively over water along river and reservoir edges. Newly volant young gray bats often feed and take shelter in forest surrounding cave entrances. Also, whenever possible, gray bats of all ages fly in the protection of forest canopy between caves and feeding areas. Such behavior provides increased protection from predators such as screech owls. Forested areas surrounding caves and between caves and over-water feeding habitat clearly are advantageous to gray bat survival. Gray bat feeding areas have not been found along sections of rivers or reservoirs where adjacent forest has been cleared.

Figure 4. Recharge zone for Logan Cave NWR showing priority areas for protection

U.S. Fish & Wildlife Service

Logan Cave National Wildlife Refuge
Benton County, Arkansas (T18N R32W)

Recharge Zone for Logan Cave NWR

Very High Priority
High Priority
Medium Priority

Date of Photography
January 24, 2006

VISITOR SERVICES

Due to intolerable disturbances to Logan Caves' protected species, the refuge is closed to all public use. Entrance into the cave by Service biologists is restricted to scientific monitoring and research activities conducted biannually, and all entry is prohibited from March through September to protect the gray bat maternity colony from disturbance. Any entrance by non-Service personnel is authorized through special use permits only. These approved activities must have approved biological and/or management implications.

The lack of exposure and awareness resulting from all activities being prohibited to the public negatively affects the Refuge's image to the local public. Environmental education and outreach is a very important tool to familiarize the local public with Logan Cave NWR and the importance of keeping the refuge closed to most activities. As part of an outreach program, refuge staff should pursue the potential of a Friends group or local volunteer(s) to provide some presence with local citizens.

SCIENTIFIC MONITORING AND RESEARCH

The wildlife species that utilize the Logan Cave NWR are so specialized that a certain amount of monitoring and research needs to be done to provide a means to assess recovery/management efforts. All monitoring and research activities need to be considered and only allowed if absolutely necessary and have approved biological and/or management implications.

REFUGE ADMINISTRATION

FUNDING AND STAFFING

Logan Cave NWR does not receive any annual funding for refuge management programs. All costs associated with the refuge are absorbed by Holla Bend NWR, which is located in Dardanelle, Arkansas, approximately 130 miles to the southeast. There is also no full-time employee assigned to the refuge.

CULTURAL RESOURCES

There have been no known official archaeological investigations within the refuge boundary.

FENCES/GATES/BOUNDARY SIGNS

One of the primary management tools for the refuge is to have the ability to keep people out of the cave to minimize disturbance to the protected species inside the cave. There are currently cave fences and gates at the spring entrance and the sinkhole to deter unauthorized access. There are also two steel gates on the north and south sides of the refuge boundary to prevent vehicle entry. Boundary signs are maintained to clearly identify the property as a national wildlife refuge that is closed to all activities. Although these things sound trivial, they are a vital part of protecting the species inhabiting Logan Cave.

WILDERNESS REVIEW

Refuge planning policy requires a wilderness review as part of the comprehensive conservation planning process. The results of the wilderness review are included in Appendix H.

IV. Management Direction

INTRODUCTION

The Service manages fish and wildlife habitats considering the needs of all resources in decision-making. But first and foremost, fish and wildlife conservation assumes priority in refuge management. A requirement of the Improvement Act is for the Service to maintain the ecological health, diversity, and integrity of refuges. Public uses are allowed if they are appropriate and compatible with wildlife and habitat conservation. The Service has identified six priority wildlife-dependent public uses. These uses are hunting, fishing, wildlife observation, wildlife photography, and environmental education and interpretation and are therefore emphasized in this CCP.

Described below is the CCP for managing the refuge over the next 15 years. This management direction contains the goals, objectives, and strategies that will be used to achieve the refuge vision.

Three alternatives for managing the refuge were considered. The Service chose Alternative 3 as the preferred management direction.

Implementing the preferred alternative will result in maintaining and enhancing water quality, flora and fauna at Logan Cave and the surrounding area, while meeting the refuge's primary purpose to protect Logan Cave's ecosystem and the threatened and endangered cave-dwelling species utilizing the cave. Specific results will add refuge staff, equipment, and funding necessary to manage, maintain, and restore the habitats and wildlife species on and off the refuge.

VISION

The vision for the refuge is as follows:

> *Logan Cave National Wildlife Refuge will maintain and enhance communities and habitats necessary for the continuing existence and recovery of federally listed endangered and threatened species. Through communication, cooperation, and consultation, the refuge will foster partnerships with private landowners and other interested parties for the conservation of important Ozark cave habitat.*

GOALS, OBJECTIVES, AND STRATEGIES

The goals, objectives, and strategies presented are the Service's response to the issues, concerns, and needs expressed by the planning team, the refuge staff and partners, and the public and are presented in hierarchical format. Chapter V, Plan Implementation, identifies the projects associated with the various strategies.

These goals, objectives, and strategies reflect the Service's commitment to achieve the mandates of the Improvement Act, the mission of the Refuge System, and the purposes and vision for Logan Cave NWR. With the resources as outlined in Chapter V, Plan Implementation, the Service intends to accomplish these goals, objectives, and strategies within the next 15 years.

GOAL 1. FISH AND WILDLIFE POPULATION MANAGEMENT

Maintain viable, historically diverse populations of native fish and wildlife species consistent with sound biological principles.

Discussion: Population management activities will focus on establishing inventorying and monitoring procedures to document species occurrence, habitat association, recruitment, and diversity. Threatened, endangered, and state identified species will be protected and managed toward recovery. All population management activities will strive to protect, maintain, and enhance species diversity in the broad context of the refuge.

Objective 1 - Benton cave crayfish: Maintain a minimum population of 35 cave crayfish based on ocular surveys.

Discussion: Provide habitat to maintain current populations of cave crayfish and establish guidelines to contribute to the recovery of the species.

Strategies:

- Perform ocular surveys bi-annually in January or February. Survey teams will be properly trained and consist of no more than four observers.

- Identify the percentage of ocular surveys that needs to be young crayfish to establish a recruitment estimate.

- Maintain water quality in Logan Cave through partnerships with landowners in the recharge zone.

- Utilize best management practices (BMPs) in recharge zone.

- Limit entry into Logan Cave to minimize disturbance to the cave crayfish.

- Identify life history and requirements for cave crayfish.

- Remove predators, if needed.

Objective 2 - Ozark Cavefish: Maintain a minimum population of 40 Ozark cavefish based on ocular surveys.

Discussion: Provide habitat to maintain current population of Ozark cavefish and establish guidelines to contribute to the recovery of the species.

Strategies:

- Perform ocular surveys bi-annually in January or February. Survey teams will be properly trained and consist of no more than four observers.

- Maintain water quality in Logan Cave through partnerships with landowners in the recharge zone.

- Utilize best management practices (BMPs) in recharge zone.

- Limit entry into Logan Cave to minimize disturbance to the cave crayfish.

- Identify the percentage of ocular surveys that needs to be young cavefish to establish a recruitment estimate.

- Identify life history and requirements for Ozark cavefish.

- Remove predators, if needed.

Objective 3 - Gray Bat: Provide habitat for a stable or increasing population of gray bats and contribute to the recovery of the species.

Strategies:

- Entry into Logan Cave must be limited (no entry from March 15-October 15) to minimize disturbance to the maternity colony.

- Perform bat guano pile surveys (for population estimates) as soon as possible after bats leave, preferably late October but no later than November 30.

- Monitor population of gray bats by performing annual exit counts in July with night vision equipment.

- Verify/identify current hibernacula used by Logan Cave gray bats.

- Continue to work with the AGFC to monitor pesticides levels in gray bats. The AGFC studied four gray bat caves in Arkansas, including Logan Cave. A breakdown product of DDT was found in samples from each cave. No other compounds were found in the samples from Logan Cave, but given the continuing influence of banned pesticides and the increasing use of new compounds in agriculture, periodic monitoring of pesticide concentrations in guano and carcasses of dead bats from Logan Cave is recommended.

Objective 4 - Indiana Bat: Provide habitat for a stable or increasing population of Indiana bats and contribute to the recovery of the species.

Discussion: Indiana bats have not been observed in Logan Cave for many years. Indiana bats use caves during hibernation from October to April, depending on climatic conditions of the cave. Summer maternity roosts are usually in trees along wooded streamside habitat.

Strategies:

- Observe/monitor for presence of Indiana bats during the crayfish/cavefish surveys.

- Study micro-climate of Logan Cave to determine suitability for Indiana bats.

Objective 5 - Other Karst Species: Maintain all populations of karst species such as pseudoscorpions, isopods, amphipods, beetles, collembolems, and other blind insects adapted to subterranean habitats.

Discussion: Maintaining these other species is vital for the continuing existence of Logan's threatened and endangered species. Many karsts species break down the raw organic energy (e.g., leaf litter and guano) to make the microorganisms that become the base of the food chain.

Strategies: All strategies for Objectives 1 and 2 apply here.

- Work in partnership with the Department of Arkansas Heritage and others to determine a complete species list that may occur in Logan Cave.

- Monitor abundance of grotto salamander.

- Identify species of special state and federal concern.

Objective 6 - Forest Dwelling Birds: Identify and implement strategies to improve forest conditions for forest dwelling birds.

Discussion: Forested habitat on Logan Cave NWR is predominantly mature oak/hickory forest. Forested habitat covers most of the refuge (approximately 100). This is small for a forested tract, but in an area where the forest is severely fragmented, it can play a large role in the presence and reproduction of forest dwelling birds. Logan Cave NWR is located within the Partners in Flight's Central Hardwoods Bird Conservation Region.

Strategies:

- Work with partners to identify avian species utilizing the refuge, including nesting species: baseline occurrence, annual, productivity, etc.

- Develop a bird list.

- Identify all refuge plant species and associations.

- Use timber stand improvement techniques to implement favorable avian habitats.

GOAL 2. HABITATS

Conserve, restore, and manage the functions and values associated with a unique karst environment in order to achieve refuge purposes and wildlife population objectives.

Discussion: Habitat management will be used to restore the biological integrity, biological diversity, and environmental health of refuge lands as well as lands within Logan Cave's recharge zone and bat foraging areas along Osage creek and other forested riparian areas used by the bats.

Objective 1 - Cave Environment: Manage the aquatic and terrestrial functions associated with this unique karst environment.

Discussion: A karst environment is influenced by many factors including but not limited to: water quantity and quality, air flow and temperature, and ground cover. These factors have changed at Logan Cave in the past 20 years, mostly by unnatural causes.

Strategies:

- Conduct cleanup inside and outside of cave. Cleanup inside (in conjunction with survey trips) to remove items left behind by trespassers, and keep debris removed from refuge property topside.

- Monitor temperature and humidity of Logan Cave.

- Stabilize sinkhole entrance.

- Perform botanical and wildlife surveys at both cave entrances.

- Monitor water quantity and quality using continuous monitoring methods and distinguish between confined and residential contaminants.

- Identify surface location of Logan Cave utilizing cave radiolocation equipment.

Objective 2 - Cave Entrances: Maintain two known entry points into Logan Cave.

Discussion: The two known entry points into Logan Cave are on refuge land, which affords the Service the opportunity to protect and monitor these entrances. Preventing trespass into the cave is imperative to the survival of the species using Logan Cave. Disturbance, especially from inexperienced cavers, can have a devastating effect on the bats, cavefish, and crayfish.

Strategies:

- Maintain bat friendly enclosures. Inspect and perform necessary maintenance at least every six months.

- Perform annual maintenance of gates and fences at cave entrances.

Objective 3 - Logan Stream (Logan Spring entrance south to refuge boundary):
Ensure water taken from the stream leaves the stream at levels (both quantity and quality) to achieve refuge purposes.

Discussion: Years ago the stream was dammed to facilitate water withdrawal from Logan Spring for the community water supply and adjacent fish farm. Today, water is still being withdrawn for private and commercial uses. Evaluate effects of water withdrawal on the cave aquatic species, especially during drought conditions. This unnatural pool of water has never been evaluated to determine if it positively or negatively affects the aquatic species in the cave. It does allow more competition/predation from epigeal crayfish and fish living in the pool.

Strategies:

- Monitor water quality and amount withdrawn from adjacent landowner using continuous monitoring methods and distinguish between confined and residential contaminants.

- Identify sensitive aquatic species in the pool.

- Remove competitors/predators if needed to protected threatened or endangered species.

Objective 4 - Bat Foraging Habitats: Explore opportunities to increase or protect important bat foraging habitat along the Osage creek corridor.

Discussion: The gray bat uses caves year-round, but when they are not hibernating, they must feed. Since gray bats forage primarily over water along rivers or lakes shores, it makes sense to protect not only the caves they utilize but also the areas where they feed.

Strategies:

- Identify important bat foraging habitats.

- Obtain FEMA floodplain map for Osage Creek to identify floodplain.

- Utilize best management practices (BMPs), and work with partners and landowners to protect and increase forested riparian corridors and improve water quality of Osage creek and its tributaries.

Objective 5 - Forest Habitat: Maintain and enhance forest habitat to allow sustained use by forest dwelling birds.

Discussion: Forested habitat at the refuge can be managed to provide different structural habitat for forest birds, and adjacent landowners can obtain assistance from federal and state agencies to enhance and increase forested habitat on their lands.

Strategy:

- Perform continuous forest inventory (or similar survey) and work with partners and landowners to provide additional forested acres surrounding the refuge, especially in the recharge zone and bat foraging areas.

GOAL 3. RESOURCE PROTECTION

Critical to the achievement of the vision for this refuge is the protection of the land and development of partnerships with landowners and conservation organizations to improve karst habitat, especially within Logan Cave's recharge zone.

Objective 1 - Recharge Zone: Protect all surface acres in the recharge zone, but focus on both the high- and very high-priority areas.

Discussion: Preventing contamination of the groundwater within the recharge zone is critical to continued existence of the aquatic species inhabiting the cave. The 1988 Federal Cave Resources Protection Act (Public Law 100-691) recognizes significant caves and establishes a formal program for federal land managers to identify, list, manage, protect, and preserve the significant caves on their lands.

Strategies:

- Identify all landowners in recharge zone.

- Establish partnerships with landowners, local governments, and land developers to implement BMP's and various land conservation programs through NRCS, TNC, NSS, AGFC, and FWS.

- Coordinate conservation efforts with Ozark Plateau NWR, Ozark Cavefish NWR, and Pilot Knob NWR across state and Service regional boundaries.

- Identify willing sellers within the recharge zone. Lands could be purchased by the FWS or cooperating agencies (i.e., The Nature Conservancy).

- Refine delineation of recharge zone.

- Evaluate road projects – Gailey Hollow road paving

- Work with Benton County and the Arkansas State Highway authorities to establish county roads within the recharge zone as "no hazardous materials" transport roads.

- Determine if Logan Cave should be officially designated as a significant cave under the 1988 FCRPA. Consider nominating if not. Utilize this designation to further cave protection, management, and preservation.

- Continue to coordinate, attend meetings, and foster partnerships within the Ozark Ecosystem.

GOAL 4. EDUCATION AND VISITOR SERVICES

Develop and implement a quality, but limited, environmental education and wildlife-dependent recreation program that would lead to a greater understanding of and appreciation for karst environments and Logan Cave's fish and wildlife resources.

Discussion: The Improvement Act identifies six priority wildlife-dependent public use activities: hunting, fishing, wildlife observation, wildlife photography, and environmental education and interpretation. Fundamental to the provision of these uses are viable and diverse fish and wildlife populations and the habitats upon which they depend. These priority uses, along with all other proposed uses, must be compatible with the refuge purpose and mission of the Refuge System. Given the sensitive nature of Logan Cave's wildlife resources, uses will be limited and focused on environmental education and interpretation.

Objective 1: Develop a community-based volunteer program and partnerships with cave-associated organizations and enthusiasts.

Discussion: Volunteers play a large role in the success of management programs on refuges across the country. They provide the eyes and ears for refuges that have administrative offices hours away from the refuge lands.

Strategies:

- Look into coordinating and partnering with the Ecological Services' program, AGFC, and others to establish and support a public use specialist position located near the refuge.

- Establish Cave Stewards (Friends Group) Program with the purpose of establishing a volunteer corps to provide visitor services for the refuge.

- Contract with a person, company, or organization located close to Logan Cave to help develop the visitor services' programs for the refuge.

- Work in partnership with cavers, local grottos, and the National Speleological Society (NSS). Utilize the national memorandum of understanding with NSS.

- Seek out and educate volunteers on karsts environments and Logan Cave management issues, etc.

- Utilize volunteers to assist with terrestrial flora and fauna surveys, and for maintenance of boundary and refuge property, etc.

Objective 2: Develop a community-based environmental education program in coordination with area schools and other area educational organizations.

Discussion: A quality environmental education program can lead to increased awareness and stewardship of the environment and can strengthen the connection between wildlife and people. It is very important to instill a land ethic in the local community and especially the local youth. Although there are limited opportunities available at Logan Cave, even a few programs can increase the local knowledge and respect for this sensitive karst ecosystem.

Strategies:

- Develop an outdoor classroom or gathering site, possibly an observation platform, where staff conducted programs allow visitors to safely view gray bats emerging from the cave's sinkhole entrance. Construct an observation platform only after refuge has been properly staffed.

- Give programs on karst environments highlighting Logan Cave NWR to local schools, adjacent landowners, county officials, 4-H groups, etc.

- Develop crayfish/cavefish brochure.

- Construct kiosk with information on karst environments and Logan Cave NWR.

Objective 3: Explore research opportunities that will assist in the recovery of threatened or endangered species utilizing the cave.

Discussion: Research on selective cave issues can lead to a better understanding of the cave environment and refuge flora and fauna, which leads to better management of the resources.

Strategies:

- Explore opportunity of completing underwater film documentary.

- Identify the life history and requirements of the cave crayfish.

- Identify the life history and requirements of the Ozark cavefish.

- Identify hibernacula used by Logan Cave gray bat maternity colony.

- Identify Logan Cave gray bat foraging habitats.

- Monitor pesticides levels in gray bats.

- Study micro-climate of the cave to determine suitability for Indiana bats.

- Refine delineation of recharge zone.

GOAL 5. REFUGE ADMINISTRATION

Provide administrative support to ensure that the goals and objectives for refuge habitats, fish and wildlife populations, land conservation, and visitor services are achieved.

Discussion: The administrative functions associated with a refuge include a wide array of activities that are critical to the mission of the Refuge System and the purpose of each refuge. These functions include staffing, training, budgeting, planning, access, law enforcement, community relations, partnering and maintenance. Refuges must have appropriate staff, facilities, equipment, and funding in order to accomplish their overall goals and objectives.

Objective 1: Develop a refuge manager position to initiate and manage the needed resource conservation projects and hire a public use specialist to develop environment education programs.

Discussion: A full-time refuge manager position is needed to oversee and conduct many of the studies, surveys, and resource protection projects identified in this CCP.

Strategies:

- Hire refuge manager (could possibly share this position with the Arkansas Ecological Services' Field Office, Holla Bend NWR, or Ozark Plateau NWR.

- Obtain operating money for Logan Cave NWR. This refuge has never been funded or received any special funds for projects.

- Hire public use specialist to develop environmental education program. This position could be shared with Holla Bend NWR, Arkansas Ecological Services Field Office, or Ozark Plateau NWR.

Objective 2: Develop effective law enforcement program to ensure trust resource protection.

Discussion: Protection of the resource is vital to the success of refuge management programs. Preventing trespass into the cave is as critical to the survival of cave species as conserving and enhancing the habitat. Collection of cavefish and crayfish for the pet industry is one factor that leads to the decline of these species. Careless spelunkers and guano harvesters disturb the gray bat maternity, increase the turbidity of the cave stream, and step on cavefish and crayfish.

Strategies:

- Initiate and complete standard operating procedures for cave search and rescue efforts.

- Utilize Service law enforcement (refuge, zone officers, and special agents) to respond to violations.

- Coordinate with AGFC wildlife officer on protocol for contacting refuge manager on issues.

- Perform surveillance as needed utilizing infra-red equipment.

- Initiate and maintain a minimum of one trip per month by refuge law enforcement officer.

V. Plan Implementation

INTRODUCTION

Refuge lands are managed as defined under the Improvement Act. Congress has distinguished a clear legislative mission of wildlife conservation for all national wildlife refuges. National wildlife refuges, unlike other public lands, are dedicated to the conservation of the Nation's fish and wildlife resources and wildlife-dependent recreational uses. Priority projects emphasize the protection and enhancement of fish and wildlife species first and foremost, but considerable emphasis is placed on balancing the needs and demands for wildlife-dependent recreation and environmental education.

To accomplish the purpose, vision, goals, and objectives contained in this plan for Logan Cave NWR, this section identifies projects, funding and personnel needs, volunteers, partnerships opportunities, step-down management plans, a monitoring and adaptive management plan, and plan review and revision.

PROPOSED PROJECTS

Listed below are the proposed project summaries and their estimated associated costs for fish and wildlife population management, habitat management, resource protection, visitor services, and refuge administration over the 15-year life of this CCP. This proposed project list reflects the priority needs identified by the public, the CCP planning team, and core refuge staff based upon available information. These projects were generated for the purpose of achieving the refuge's objectives and strategies (Table 1). The primary linkages of these projects to those planning elements are identified in each summary under the project category.

FISH AND WILDLIFE POPULATION MANAGEMENT

Project 1: Science-based Inventory and Monitoring of Refuge Flora and Fauna

Science-based inventories and monitoring of plant and animal populations are critical to ensuring the biological integrity of the refuge. Information collected will serve as the basis for developing habitat management plans and will influence all management activities. A systematic inventory and monitoring program will enable the refuge to make informed management decisions and valuable long-term contributions to national and regional objectives for threatened and endangered species and resident wildlife. All data will be shared with appropriate state and federal partners in an effort to further ecosystem management. A monitoring plan should be developed to describe survey methods, survey duration, and frequency of sampling to keep surveys of Logan Cave NWR's species consistent through the years during staff and partners' changes. The monitoring plan must incorporate ways to minimize turbidity during surveys inside the cave; list needed participants and limits to cave entry. Benton cave crayfish monitoring should be incorporated into Ozark cavefish surveys. The estimated first-year cost for this project is $20,000, with a recurring cost of $ 2,000 per year. *(Linkages: Goal 1, Objectives 1, 2, 3 4, 5, and 6; Goal 2, Objectives 1,2,3,4, and 5.)*

Project 2: Identify Life History and Requirements for Amblyopsis rosae and Cambarus aculabrum for the Logan Cave system.

Little is known about the ecology and natural history of troglobitic crayfish, and only limited observations have been made of *Cambarus aculabrum*. Population levels are too low to risk individuals in studies that may result in mortality. Studies, such as species habitat utilization, fecundity, mortality rate, longevity, food preference, etc., should only be initiated when it is determined that such studies will have no impact on the ability of the species to survive. Notes on behavior, location, and reproductive status should be taken of any observations of cave crayfish made during survey trips. Much is known about *Amblyopsis rosae*, but little is known about what is required for successful reproduction of these fish. Spawning is likely triggered by spring floods. Gravid females have been observed in Logan Cave during the month of January when the lowest flows of the year are recorded. In many caves, the greatest obstacle may be finding potential mates at the right time. Studies are needed to determine the extent of competition and predation on *A. rosae and C. aculabrum* by troglophilic and epigeal species at Logan Cave. Biannual surveys of troglophiles and epigeans should be conducted in such a way that they do not harm *A. rosae* and *C. aculabrum*.

The estimated first-year cost for this project is $20,000, with recurring cost of $5,000 for study duration. (*Linkages: Goal 1, Objectives 1and 2*)

Project 3: Purchase Night Vision Equipment to Monitor Gray Bats

Night vision/infrared equipment is needed to perform consistent exit counts of the Logan Cave gray bat maternity colony. Two sets of night vision equipment are needed to monitor both entrances at the same time. Currently only one survey is performed by an AGFC contractor. Monthly surveys are needed during late spring and through the summer to monitor bat presence and possible disturbance to the maternity colony. The estimated cost for this equipment is $10,000. (*Linkage: Goal 1, Objective 3*)

Project 4: Conduct Banding/Monitoring Study to Verify/Identify Hibernacula used by Logan Cave Gray Bat Colony

The hibernacula and transient locations used by Logan Cave gray bats are unknown. Knowing where this population of bats spends the winter and their migration routes will allow the Service and partners to initiate plans to protect these areas. The refuge would work with AGFC and other Service biologists to accomplish this project. The estimated first-year cost for this project is $ 3,000, with recurring cost of $1,000 each year for an approximate 5-year study. (*Linkage: Goal 1, Objective 3*)

Project 5: Identify Logan Cave Gray Bat Foraging Areas

Gray bats feed primarily over water along river, stream, and reservoir edges and in forest canopy along waters edge and take flight in the protection of the forest canopy between the cave and feeding areas to avoid predators. Gray bat feeding areas have not been found along sections of river or reservoir where adjacent forest has been cleared. Identifying the current feeding areas and forested corridors is imperative to the existence of the Logan Cave gray bat colony. Once these areas are identified, steps can be taken through partnerships with landowners to protect and enhance these forested areas. The estimated first-year cost for this project is $15,000, with recurring cost of $5,000. (*Linkages: Goal 1, Objective 3 and 4; Goal 2, Objective 4*)

Project 6: Determine Suitability of Logan Cave for Indiana bat

Indiana bats could once be found hibernating in Logan Cave. Indiana bats have specific needs for cave temperatures during hibernation. Changes in the air flow through caves can change the temperature enough to make it unsuitable for Indiana bats. The air flow through Logan Cave has changed significantly over the past 20 years due to erosion at the sinkhole entrance, which has almost closed it completely. Temperature and humidity data loggers should be installed and monitored to record specific conditions inside the cave to determine if it is suitable for Indiana bats. The estimated first-year cost for this project is $ 5,000, with a recurring cost of $ 500. (*Linkages: Goal 1, Objectives 3 and 4; Goal 2, Objective*1)

HABITAT MANAGEMENT

Project 7: Monitor Water Quantity and Quality of Logan Cave Stream and Spring

Degradation of water quality poses the greatest threat to the aquatic species of Logan Cave. Water quality data needed include pH, water and air temperature, turbidity, dissolved oxygen, biological oxygen demand, dissolved organic carbon, conductivity, total dissolved and suspended solids, nitrates, metals, and pesticides. The cave stream and spring should be sampled monthly for at least one year to establish a baseline for future comparisons. Metals should be sampled once for baseline and additional tests if warranted. Testing for pesticides, insecticides, or lawn chemicals should be done after a rainfall of at least one inch. Data needs to be gathered on anthropogenic enrichment and organic loading of Logan Cave.

Water quantity also plays an important role in the survival of the cave's aquatic species. Past and future increases in the utilization of the water from the cave will have an impact on water levels in the cave, especially during periods of drought. Unnatural decreases in water levels in the cave stream could have an adverse impact on the cave's aquatic habitat. The amount of water removed and its affects on the cave's aquatic species and climate should be monitored. The estimated first-year cost for this project is $20,000, with recurring cost of $5,000. (*Linkages: Goal 2, Objective 1 and 3*)

Project 8: Initiate Sinkhole Stabilization Project Utilizing USGS Data

In 2004, the USGS studied the geologic conditions at the sinkhole entrance to Logan Cave and recommended that the sinkhole be protected from foot traffic and the slope be stabilized to lessen the erosion, which could lead to complete filling of the sinkhole by sediments. Sedimentation around sinkholes of caves is normal. But the sinkhole entrance of Logan Cave has had a significant amount of sediment mainly from foot traffic (trespass) from the top of the sink to the bottom of the slope which has almost completely blocked the entrance. Recent fencing of the sinkhole has significantly reduced foot traffic, but current sediments need to be removed and the slope around the foot trail stabilized to reduce further unnatural erosion. The estimated first year cost for this project is $5,000, with recurring cost of $500 (*Linkage: Goal 2, Objective 2*)

RESOURCE PROTECTION

Project 9: Utilize Cave Radiolocation to Locate and Map Cave to Surface Relationship

Cave radiolocation is a technique used to locate sections of a cave from the surface. The techniques and equipment used allow researchers to map the cave passages and related those passages to the surface. Knowing where the cave passages lay from the surface will greatly enhance the ability of management to protect the cave through partnerships with landowners and will aid rescuers in the event of an incident. Current and future landowners will know if cave passages lie under their land before engaging in land activities that could seriously affect the cave environment. The estimated cost for this project is $5,000. (*Linkages: Goal 2, Objective 1; Goal 3, Objective 1; Goal 5, Objective 2*)

Project 10: Increase Resource Protection by Purchasing Specialized Surveillance Equipment for Law Enforcement

This project would provide funding for purchasing state-of-the-art surveillance equipment for refuge law enforcement officers to increase the protection of the cave's natural resources. This equipment would also be used to assist local partners with cave resource protection projects. The estimated cost is $8,000. (*Linkage: Goal 5, Objective 2*)

VISITOR SERVICES

Project 11: Develop Logan Cave Brochure

Due to Logan Cave's sensitive fauna, no outreach occurs at or in the cave proper. Developing a general brochure that gives information and pictures about the cave environment and refuge flora and fauna would be an excellent outreach tool to hand out at local events and have available via the Internet. The estimated first-year cost for this project is $3,000, with periodic cost of approximately $600 for additional brochures as needed. (*Linkages: Goal 4, Objective 2*)

Project 12: Construct Viewing Platform

During the summer months, bats can easily be seen exiting the cave's sinkhole entrance at dusk to forage. The cave is fenced and gated and closed to all public entry. If a public use specialist or manager were to be hired, a viewing platform near the sinkhole entrance could be used for scheduled interpretation and educational activities for local youth groups, clubs, and partners. The estimated first-year cost of this project is $20,000, with a recurring cost of $500. (*Linkages: Goal 4, Objective 2*)

Project 13. Construct Kiosks

A wooden kiosk would be constructed at the north entrance gate for year-round information on Logan Cave NWR and its resources. The estimated first-year cost of this project is $10,000, with a recurring cost of $500. (*Linkages: Goal 4, Objective 2*)

REFUGE ADMINISTRATION

Project 14: Manage Endangered Wildlife and Habitats by Re-establishing the Refuge Manager Position

In 1994, during staff reductions, the refuge manager position for Logan Cave NWR was lost. This project would re-establish this position to oversee the management of Logan Cave NWR and carry out many of the biological surveys and possibly assist with coordinating other Service cave and karst related acitivties in the Arkansas Ozarks. This position could be stationed at the Complex headquarters (Holla Bend NWR), as in the past, or shared with Ozark Plateau NWR, the Conway, AR or Tulsa, OK Ecological Services' offices. The estimated first-year cost for this project is $160,000, with recurring cost of $89,000. (*Linkages: Goal 5, Objective 1*)

Project 15: Hire Public Use Specialist

This project would involve hiring a public use specialist to coordinate and perform outreach for the refuge and surrounding karst environment. This position could be stationed at the Complex headquarters (Holla Bend NWR) and would be responsible for all of Logan Cave NRW environmental education programs. The estimated first-year cost for this project is $160,000, with recurring cost of $70,000. (*Linkage: Goal 5, Objective 1*)

FUNDING AND PERSONNEL

To complete the wildlife and habitat management projects and conduct the necessary inventorying, monitoring, analysis, mapping, and outreach activities, staff is required. Logan Cave NWR has never been staffed or received resource management funding. The planning team and the public identified the need for staff at Logan Cave NWR. The proposed positions listed above are needed for the refuge to achieve its plan objectives and strategies. The annual estimated cost of operating the refuge, including salaries and benefits of the two positions listed above, will be $160,000.

PARTNERSHIP/VOLUNTEERS OPPORTUNITIES

A key element of this CCP is to establish partnerships with local volunteers, landowners, private organizations, and state and federal natural resource agencies. In the immediate vicinity of the refuge, opportunities exist to establish partnerships with local landowners, 4-H and scout groups, land developers, caving clubs, and Audubon groups. At regional and state levels, partnerships may be established or enhanced with organizations such as The Nature Conservancy, Natural Resources Conservation Agency, the National Speleological Society, Arkansas Game and Fish Commission, USDA Forest Service, and the University of Arkansas at Fayetteville.

STEP-DOWN MANAGEMENT PLANS

A CCP is a strategic plan that guides the future direction of the refuge. A step-down management plan provides specific guidance on activities, such as habitat, fire, and visitor services management. These plans (Table 2) are also developed in accordance with NEPA, which requires the identification and evaluation of alternatives and public review and involvement prior to their implementation.

MONITORING AND ADAPTIVE MANAGEMENT

Adaptive management is a flexible approach to long-term management of biotic resources that is directed over time by the results of ongoing monitoring activities and other information. More specifically, adaptive management is a process by which projects are implemented within a framework of scientifically driven experiments to test the predictions and assumptions outlined within a plan.

To apply adaptive management, specific survey, inventory, and monitoring protocols will be adopted for the refuge. The habitat management strategies will be systematically evaluated to determine management effects on wildlife populations. This information will be used to refine approaches and determine how effectively the objectives are being accomplished. Evaluations will include ecosystem team and other appropriate partner participation. If monitoring and evaluation indicate undesirable effects for target and non-target species and/or communities, then alterations to the management projects will be made. Subsequently, this CCP will be revised. Specific monitoring and evaluation activities will be described in the step-down management plans.

Table 1. Summary of projects

PROJECT NUMBER	PROJECT TITLE	FIRST YEAR COST	RECURRING ANNUAL COST	STAFF (FTE'S)
1	Science-based Inventory and Monitoring of Refuge Flora and Fauna	$20,000	$2,000	
2	Identify Life History and Requirements for A. rosae and C. aculabrum for the Logan Cave system.	$20,000	$5,000 **	
3	Purchase Night Vision Equipment to Monitor Gray Bats	$10,000	*	
4	Conduct Study to Identify Hibernacula Used by Logan Cave Gray Bat Colony	$ 3,000	$1,000 **	
5	Identify Logan Cave Gray Bat Foraging Areas	$15,000	$5,000 **	
6	Determine Suitability of Logan Cave for Indiana Bats	$ 5,000	$ 500	
7	Monitor Water Quantity and Quality of Logan Stream and Spring	$20,000	$5,000	
8	Initiate Sinkhole Stabilization Project	$5,000	$500	
9	Utilize Cave Radiolocation to Locate and Map Cave to Surface Relationship	$5,000	*	
10	Purchase Surveillance Equipment for Law Enforcement	$8,000	*	
11	Develop and Print Logan Cave Brochure	$ 3,000	$ 600	
12	Construct Viewing Platform	$ 20,000	$ 500	
13	Construct Kiosk	$ 10,000	$ 500	
14	Re-establish Refuge Manager Position	$160,000	$89,000	1
15	Hire Public Use Specialist	$160,000	$70,000	1
Grand Total		$ 464,000	$ 168,600	2

* No recurring cost.
** Recurring cost for duration of the study and not included in total recurring costs.

PLAN REVIEW AND REVISION

This CCP will be reviewed annually in development of the refuge's annual work plans and budget. It will also be reviewed to determine the need for revision. A revision will occur if and when conditions change or significant information becomes available, such as a change in ecological conditions or a major refuge expansion. This CCP will be augmented by detailed step-down management plans to address the completion of specific strategies in support of the refuge's goals and objectives. Revisions to the CCP and the step-down management plans will be subject to public review and NEPA compliance.

Table 2. Logan Cave National Wildlife Refuge step-down management plans related to the goals and objectives of the CCP

Step-down Plan	Completion Date
Wildlife Management Plan	2012
Biological Inventory/Monitoring Plan	2010
Nuisance Animal Control	2012
Exotic Plant Control	2012
Habitat Management Plan	2012
Water Quality and Quantity Monitoring Plan	2010
Forest Management Plan	2012
Law Enforcement	2010
Safety/Search and Rescue Plan	2010
Visitor Services	2015
Environmental Education and Interpretation	2015

Appendix A. Glossary

Adaptive Management:
Refers to a process in which policy decisions are implemented within a framework of scientifically driven experiments to test predictions and assumptions inherent in management plan. Analysis of results help managers determine whether current management should continue as is or whether it should be modified to achieve desired conditions.

Allochthonous:
Organic matter synthesized within a drainage basin and brought to lakes or streams in various forms of detritus.

Anthropogenic:
A term that refers to the environmental effects, processes or materials causes from the chemical or biological wastes that are produced from human activities.

Aquifer:
Underground water contained in water-holding geological layers.

Best Management Practices (BMP's):
Practices determined by state and federal agencies to be the most effective and practical means of preventing or reducing the amount of water pollution generated by various land uses and construction.

Biological Diversity:
The variety of life and its processes, including the variety of living organisms, the genetic differences among them, and the communities and ecosystems in which they occur (USFWS Manual 052 FW 1. 12B). The System's focus is on indigenous species, biotic communities, and ecological processes. Also referred to as Biodiversity.

BOD:
The biological oxygen demand (BOD) is an approximate measure of the amount of biochemically degradable organic matter present in a water sample.

Carrying Capacity:
The maximum population of a species able to be supported by a habitat or area.

Categorical Exclusion (CE,CX, CATEX, CATX):
A category of actions that do not individually or cumulatively have a significant effect on the human environment and have been found to have no such effect in procedures adopted by a Federal agency pursuant to the National Environmental Policy Act (40 CFR 1508.4).

CFR:
Code of Federal Regulations.

Compatible Use: A proposed or existing wildlife-dependent recreational use or any other use of a national wildlife refuge that, based on sound professional judgment, will not materially interfere with or detract from the fulfillment of the National Wildlife Refuge System mission or the purpose(s) of the national wildlife refuge (50 CFR 25.12 (a)). A compatibility determination supports the selection of compatible uses and identifies stipulations or limits necessary to ensure compatibility.

Comprehensive Conservation Plan (CCP): A document that describes the desired future conditions of a refuge or planning unit and provides long-range guidance and management direction to achieve the purposes of the refuge; helps fulfill the mission of the Refuge System; maintains and, where appropriate, restores the ecological integrity of each refuge and the Refuge System; helps achieve the goals of the National Wilderness Preservation System; and meets other mandates (Service Manual 602 FW 1.6 E).

Concern: See Issue.

Conservation: Conserving natural resources for future generations while using them wisely, as opposed to exploitation or total nonuse.

Conservation Easement: A legal agreement with a property owner to restrict the clearing of habitat, construction, or other activities within a specified zone which may be detrimental to wildlife, or their habitat, in return for financial benefit such as a payment of an income or estate tax reduction.

Cover: Vegetation used by wildlife for protection from predators or to escape the adverse effects of weather.

Cultural Resource Inventory: A professionally conducted study designed to locate and evaluate evidence of cultural resources present within a defined geographic area. Inventories may involve various levels, including background literature search, comprehensive field examination to identify all exposed physical manifestations of cultural resources, or sample inventory to project site distribution and density over a larger area. Evaluation of identified cultural resources to determine eligibility for the National Register follows the criteria found in 36 CFR 60.4 (Service Manual 614 FW 1.7).

Cultural Resource Overview: A comprehensive document prepared for a field office that discusses, among other things, its prehistory and cultural history, the nature and extent of known cultural resources, previous research, management objectives, resource management conflicts or issues, and a general statement on how program objectives should be met and conflicts resolved. An overview should reference or incorporate information from a field offices background or literature search described in Section VIII of the Cultural Resource Management Handbook (Service Manual 614 FW 1.7).

Cultural Resources:	The remains of sites, structures, or objects used by people in the past.
Detritus:	Dead or decaying organic matter.
Disturbance:	Significant alteration of habitat structure or composition. May be natural (e.g., fire) or human-caused events (e.g., aircraft overflight).
Ecoregion:	Ecological region as determined by the Service, but defined by geographic similarities.
Ecosystem:	A dynamic and interrelating complex of plant and animal communities and their associated non-living environment.
Ecosystem Management:	Management of natural resources using system-wide concepts to ensure that all plants and animals in ecosystems are maintained at viable levels in native habitats and basic ecosystem processes are perpetuated indefinitely.
Endangered Species (Federal):	A plant or animal species listed under the Endangered Species Act that is in danger of extinction throughout all or a significant portion of its range.
Endangered Species (State):	A plant or animal species in danger of becoming extinct or extirpated in the state within the near future if factors contributing to its decline continue. Populations of these species are at critically low levels or their habitats have been degraded or depleted to a significant degree.
Endemic:	Native or confined to a certain region; having a comparatively restricted distribution.
Environmental Assessment (EA):	A concise public document, prepared in compliance with the National Environmental Policy Act, that briefly discusses the purpose and need for an action, alternatives to such action, and provides sufficient evidence and analysis of impacts to determine whether to prepare an environmental impact statement or finding of no significant impact (40 CFR 1508.9).
Environmental Impact Statement (EIS):	A detailed written statement required by section 102(2)(C) of the National Environmental Policy Act, analyzing the environmental impacts of a proposed action, adverse effects of the project that cannot be avoided, alternative courses of action, short-term uses of the environment versus the maintenance and enhancement of long-term productivity, and any irreversible and irretrievable commitment of resources (40 CFR 1508.11).
Epigeal:	A term that refers to species that live or grow on or right above the surface of the ground.

Exotic:	A plant or animal species not native to the area and introduced intentionally or unintentionally.
Fauna:	Animals, including lesser forms such as insects, mites, etc.
Finding of No Significant Impact (FONSI):	A document prepared in compliance with the National Environmental Policy Act, supported by an environmental assessment, that briefly presents why a Federal action will have no significant effect on the human environment and for which an environmental impact statement, therefore, will not be prepared (40 CFR 1508.13).
Flora:	Plants and trees.
Floodplain:	The flat floor of a valley which is periodically flooded by a river.
Forage Areas:	Vegetated areas with some degree of canopy closure of tree and tall shrubs (greater than seven feet in height).
Goal:	Descriptive, open-ended, and often broad statement of desired future conditions that conveys a purpose but does not define measurable units (Service Manual 620 FW 1.6J).
Habitat:	Suite of existing environmental conditions required by an organism for survival and reproduction. The place where an organism typically lives.
Habitat Restoration:	Management emphasis designed to move ecosystems to desired conditions and processes, and/or to healthy ecosystems.
Habitat Type:	An aggregation of all land areas potentially capable of producing similar plant communities at climax stage.
Hibernacula:	Places where bats hibernate over the winter.
Improvement Act:	The National Wildlife Refuge System Improvement Act of 1997.
Invertebrates:	Animals without a backbone, such as insects or snails.
Issue:	Any unsettled matter that requires a management decision, e.g., an initiative, opportunity, resource management problem, threat to the resources of the unit, conflict in uses, public concern, or other presence of an undesirable resource condition (Service Manual 602 FW 1.6K).

Management Alternative:	See Alternative
Management Concern:	See Issue
Management Opportunity:	See Issue
Maternity Cave:	Cave used by bats to raise their young.
Migration:	The seasonal movement from one area to another and back.
Mission Statement:	Succinct statement of the unit's purpose and reason for being.
Monitoring:	The process of collecting information to track changes of selected parameters over time.
National Environmental Policy Act of 1969 (NEPA):	Requires all agencies, including the Service, to examine the environmental impacts of their actions, incorporate environmental information, and use public participation in the planning and implementation of all actions. Federal agencies must integrate NEPA with other planning requirements, and prepare appropriate NEPA documents to facilitate better environmental decision making (40 CFR 1500).
National Wildlife Refuge System Improvement Act of 1997 (Public Law 105-57):	Under the Improvement Act, the Service is required to develop 15-year comprehensive conservation plans for all national wildlife refuges outside Alaska. The Act also describes the six public uses given priority status within the NWRS (i.e., hunting, fishing, wildlife observation, wildlife photography, and environmental education and interpretation).
National Wildlife Refuge System Mission:	The mission is to administer a national network of lands and waters for the conservation, management, and where appropriate, restoration of the fish, wildlife, and plant resources and their habitats within the United States for the benefit of present and future generations of Americans.
National Wildlife Refuge System:	Various categories of areas administered by the Secretary of the Interior for the conservation of fish and wildlife, including species threatened with extinction; all lands, waters, and interests therein administered by the Secretary as wildlife refuges; areas for the protection and conservation of fish and wildlife that are threatened with extinction; wildlife ranges; games ranges; wildlife management areas; or waterfowl production areas.

National Wildlife Refuge:	A designated area of land, water, or an interest in land or water within the System.
Native Species:	Species that normally live and thrive in a particular ecosystem.
Neotropical Migratory Birds:	Numerous species of birds that spend the winter in the Caribbean, Central and South America and migrate in the springtime across the Gulf of Mexico to their breeding and nesting areas in North America.
Notice of Intent (NOI):	A notice that an environmental impact statement will be prepared and considered (40 CFR 1508.22). Published in the *Federal Register*.
Noxious Weed:	A plant species designated by federal or state law as generally possessing one or more of the following characteristics: aggressive or difficult to manage; parasitic; a carrier or host of serious insect or disease; or non-native, new, or not common to the United States, according to the Federal Noxious Weed Act (PL 93-639), a noxious weed is one that causes disease or had adverse effects on man or his environment and therefore is detrimental to the agriculture and commerce of the Untied States and to the public health.
Objective:	A concise statement of what we want to achieve, how much we want to achieve, when and where we want to achieve it, and who is responsible for the work. Objectives derive from goals and provide the basis for determining strategies, monitoring refuge accomplishments, and evaluating the success of strategies. Making objectives attainable, time-specific, and measurable (Service Manual 602 FW 1.6N).
Plant Association:	A classification of plant communities based on the similarity in dominants of all layers of vascular species in a climax community.
Plant Community:	An assemblage of plant species unique in its composition; occurs in particular locations under particular influences; a reflection or integration of the environmental influences on the site such as soils, temperature, elevation, solar radiation, slope, aspect, and rainfall; denotes a general kind of climax plant community.
Preferred Alternative:	This is the alternative determined [by the decision maker] to best achieve the refuge purpose, vision, and goals; contributes to the Refuge System mission, addresses the significant issues; and is consistent with principles of sound fish and wildlife management.

Priority Species: Fish and wildlife species that the Service believes require protective measures and/or management guidelines to ensure their perpetuation. Priority species include the following: (1) state-listed and candidate species; (2) species or groups of animals susceptible to significant population declines within a specific area or statewide by virtue of their inclination to aggregate (e.g., seabird colonies); and (3) species of recreation, commercial, and/or tribal importance.

Public Involvement Plan: Broad long-term guidance for involving the public in the comprehensive planning process.

Public Involvement: A process that offers impacted and interested individuals and organizations an opportunity to become informed about, and to express their opinions on Service actions and policies. In the process, these views are studied thoroughly and thoughtful consideration of public views is given in shaping decisions for refuge management.

Public: Individuals, organizations, and groups; officials of federal, state, and local government agencies; Indian tribes; and foreign nations. It may include anyone outside the core planning team. It includes those who may or may not have indicated an interest in service issues and those who do or do not realize that Service decisions may affect them.

Purposes of the Refuge: "The purposes specified in or derived from the law, proclamation, executive order, agreement, public land order, donation document, or administrative memorandum establishing, authorizing, or expanding a refuge, refuge unit, or refuge sub-unit." For refuges that encompass congressionally designated wilderness, the purposes of the Wilderness Act are additional purposes of the refuge (Service Manual 602 FW 106 S).

Recharge Zone: The surface and groundwater regions that contribute water to Logan Cave stream and spring.

Record of Decision (ROD): A concise public record of decision prepared by the federal agency, pursuant to NEPA, that contains a statement of the decision, identification of all alternatives considered, identification of the environmentally preferable alternative, a statement as to whether all practical means to avoid or minimize environmental harm from the alternative selected have been adopted (and if not, why they were not), and a summary of monitoring and enforcement where applicable for any mitigation (40 CFR 1505.2).

Reforestation: The natural or artificial restocking of an area with forest trees.

Refuge Goal: See Goal.

Refuge Purposes:	See Purposes of the refuge.
Riparian:	Of or relating to land lying immediately adjacent to a water body and having specific characteristics of that transitional area, such as riparian vegetation. A stream bank is an example of a riparian area.
Roost Caves:	Caves used by bats to sleep during the day or when they are not feeding.
Sinkhole:	A depression in the ground
Songbirds: (Also Passerines)	A category of birds that is medium to small, perching land birds. Most are territorial singers and migratory.
Step-down Management Plan:	A plan that provides specific guidance on management subjects (e.g., habitat, public use, fire, safety) or groups of related subjects. It describes strategies and implementation schedules for meeting CCP goals and objectives (Service Manual 602 FW 1.6 U).
Strategy:	A specific action, tool, technique, or combination of actions, tools, and techniques used to meet unit objectives (Service Manual 602 FW 1.6 U).
Study Area:	The area reviewed in detail for wildlife, habitat, and public use potential. For purposes of this CCP/EIS, the study area includes the lands within the currently approved refuge boundary and potential refuge expansion areas.
Threatened Species (Federal):	Species listed under the Endangered Species Act that are likely to become endangered within the foreseeable future throughout all or a significant portion of their range.
Threatened Species (State):	A plant or animal species likely to become endangered in the state within the near future if factors contributing to population decline or habitat degradation or loss continue.
Tiering:	The coverage of general matters in broader environmental impact statements with subsequent narrower statements of environmental analysis, incorporating by reference, the general discussions and concentrating on specific issues (40 CFR 1508.28).
Troglobites	A term used to refer to cave-adapted species that show lack of eyes and pigmentation, with greater development of other sensory organs.

Troglophiles	Species that are commonly found in caves but are also found in suitable habitats on the surface.
U.S. Fish and Wildlife Service Mission:	The mission of the U.S. Fish and Wildlife Service is working with others to conserve, protect, and enhance fish and wildlife and their habitats for the continuing benefit of the American people.
Unit Objective:	See Objective.
Vegetation Type, Habitat Type, Forest Cover Type:	A land classification system based upon the concept of distinct plant associations.
Vision Statement:	A concise statement of what the planning unit should be, or what we hope to do, based primarily upon the Refuge System mission and specific refuge purposes, and other mandates. We will tie the vision statement for the refuge to the mission of the Refuge System; the purpose(s) of the refuge; the maintenance or restoration of the ecological integrity of each refuge and the Refuge System; and other mandates (Service Manual 602 FW 1.6 Z).
Watershed:	The entire land area that collects and drains water into a stream or stream system.
Wildfire:	A free-burning fire requiring a suppression response; all fire other than prescribed fire that occurs on wildlands (Service Manual 621 FW 1.7).
Wildland Fire:	Every wildland fire is either a wildfire or a prescribed fire (Service Manual 621 FW 1.3).

ACRONYMS AND ABBREVIATIONS

AGFC	Arkansas Game and Fish Commission
CCP	Comprehensive Conservation Plan
CFR	Code of Federal Regulations
DOI	Department of Interior
EA	Environmental Assessment
EIS	Environmental Impact Statement
EPA	U.S. Environmental Protection Agency
ESA	Endangered Species Act
FONSI	Finding of No Significant Impact
FR	Federal Register
FTE	Full-time equivalent
FY	Fiscal Year
GIS	Global Information System
NEPA	National Environmental Policy Act
NRCS	Natural Resource Conservation Service
NRHP	National Register of Historic Places
NSS	National Speleological Society
NWR	National Wildlife Refuge
NWRS	National Wildlife Refuge System
PFT	Permanent Full Time
RM	Refuge Manual
ROD	Record of Decision
Service	U.S. Fish and Wildlife Service (also, FWS)
TFT	Temporary Full Time
TNC	The Nature Conservancy
USC	United States Code
USFWS	U.S. Fish and Wildlife Service

Appendix B. References and Literature Citations

Aley, T. and Aley, C. 1987. Final Report: Water quality protection studies for Logan Cave, Arkansas. Ozark Underground Laboratory contract report to Arkansas Game and Fish Commission and U.S. Fish and Wildlife Service. 61pp. + Tables and Maps.

Arkansas Game and Fish Commission. 2005, Revised 2006. The Arkansas Comprehensive Wildlife Conservation Strategy. 1647 pp. + appendices.

Boyd, Gianetta L. 1997. Metabolic Rates and Life History of Aquatic Organisms Inhabiting Logan Cave Stream in Northwest Arkansas. M.S. Thesis. 107pp.

Brown, Arthur V. 1980. A Proposal to Purchase Logan Cave and the Accompanying Property in Benton, County, Arkansas. Unpublished Document, University of Arkansas Fayetteville, 21pp.

Means, Myron L. 1993. Population Dynamics and Movement of Ozark Cavefish in Logan Cave National Wildlife Refuge, Benton County, Arkansas, with Additional Baseline Water Quality Information. M.S. Thesis. University of Arkansas, Fayetteville, Arkansas. 126pp.

Partners in Amphibian and Reptile Conservation (PARC). 2004. PARC Brochure. Accessed online 5-31-07 at http://www.parcplace.org/publications.html#about.

Schultz, William H., and McKenna, Jonathan P. 2004. Engineering Geologic Conditions at the Sinkhole Entrance to Logan Cave, Benton County, Arkansas. U. S. Geological Survey Open-File Report 2004-1357. 15pp. + App and Maps.

Sasse, Blake D. 2005. Pesticide Residues in Guano of Gray Bats in Arkansas. Journal of the Arkansas Academy of Science. Vol. 59: pp. 214-217.

The Nature Conservancy, Ozarks Ecoregional Assessment Team. 2003. Ozarks Ecoregional Conservation Assessment. Minneapolis, MN: The Nature Conservancy Midwestern Resource Office. 48 pp. + 5 appendices.

U.S. Census Bureau, 2006. Accessed online 5-18-2007 at http://www.factfinder.census.gov.

U.S. Fish and Wildlife Service. 1982. Gray Bat Recovery Plan. Prepared by the U.S. Fish and Wildlife Service in cooperation with the Gray Bat Recovery Team. 17 pp. + App.

U.S. Fish and Wildlife Service. 1989. Ozark Cavefish Recovery Plan. U.S. Fish and Wildlife Service. Atlanta, Georgia. 15pp.

U.S. Fish and Wildlife Service. 1996. Cave crayfish (*Cambarus aculabrum*) Recovery Plan. Atlanta, Georgia. 37pp.

U.S. Fish and Wildlife Service. 1999. Agency Draft Indiana Bat (*Myotis sodalis*) Revised Recovery Plan. Fort Snelling, Minnesota. 53pp.

U.S. Fish and Wildlife Service. 2002. Ozark Plateau National Wildlife Refuge Proposed Refuge Expansion Environmental Assessment.

U.S. Fish and Wildlife Service. 2005. Draft Comprehensive Conservation Plan and Environmental Assessment. Lake Ophelia National Wildlife Refuge.

U.S. Fish and Wildlife Service. 2005. Community Growth Best Management Practices for Conservation of the Cave Springs Cave Recharge Zone. Prepared by David Kampwerth, USFWS, Arkansas Field Office. Conway, Arkansas. 14pp.

Appendix C. Relevant Legal Mandates and Executive Orders

Administrative Procedures Act (1946)	Outlines administrative procedures to be followed by Federal agencies with respect to identification of information to be made public; publication of material in the Federal Register; maintenance of records; attendance and notification requirements for specific meetings and hearings; issuance of licenses; and review of agency actions.
American Antiquities Act of 1906	Provides penalties for unauthorized collection, excavation, or destruction of historic or prehistoric ruins, monuments, or objects of antiquity on lands owned or controlled by the United States. The Act authorizes the President to designate as national monuments objects or areas of historic or scientific interest on lands owned or controlled by the Unites States.
American Indian Religious Freedom Act of 1978	Protects the inherent right of Native Americans to believe, express, and exercise their traditional religions, including access to important sites, use and possession of sacred objects, and the freedom to worship through ceremonial and traditional rites.
Americans With Disabilities Act of 1990	Prevents discrimination of and makes American Society more accessible to people with disabilities. The Act requires reasonable accommodations to be made in employment, public services, public accommodations, and telecommunications for persons with disabilities.
Archaeological Resources Protection Act of 1979, as amended.	Strengthens and expands the protective provisions of the Antiquities Act of 1906 regarding archaeological resources. It also revised the permitting process for archaeological research.
Architectural Barriers Act of 1968	Requires that buildings and facilities designed, constructed, or altered with Federal funds, or leased by a Federal agency comply with standards for physical accessibility.
Bald and Golden Eagle Protection Act of 1940, as amended	Prohibits the possession, sale, or transport of any bald or golden eagle, alive or dead, or part, nest, or egg except as permitted by the Secretary of the Interior for scientific or exhibition purposes, or for the religious purposes of Indians.
Bankhead-Jones Farm Tenant Act of 1937	Directs the Secretary of Agriculture to develop a program of land conservation and utilization in order to correct maladjustments in land use and thus assist in such things as control of soil erosion, reforestation, conservation of natural resources, and protection of fish and wildlife. Some early refuges and hatcheries were established under authority of this Act.
Cave Resources Protection Act of 1988	Established requirements for the management and protection of caves and their resources on Federal lands, including allowing the land managing agencies to withhold the location of caves from the public, and requiring permits for any removal or collecting activities in caves on Federal lands.

Clean Air Act of 1970	Regulates air emissions from area, stationary, and mobile sources. This Act and its amendments charge Federal land managers with direct responsibility to protect the "air quality and related values" of land under their control. These values include fish, wildlife, and their habitats.
Clean Water Act of 1974, as amended	This Act has as its objective the restoration and maintenance of the chemical, physical, and biological integrity of the Nation's waters. Section 401 of the Act requires that federally permitted activities comply with the Clean Water Act standards, State water quality laws, and any other appropriate State laws. Section 404 charges the U.S. Army Corps of Engineers with regulating discharge of dredge or fill materials into waters of the United States, including wetlands.
Emergency Wetlands Resources Act of 1986	Authorized the purchase of wetlands from Land and Water Conservation Fund moneys, removing a prior prohibition on such acquisitions. The Act requires the Secretary to establish a National Wetlands Priority Conservation Plan, requires States to include wetlands in their Comprehensive Outdoor Recreation Plans, and transfers to the Migratory Bird Conservation Fund amounts equal to import duties on arms and ammunition. It also established entrance fees at national wildlife refuges.
Endangered Species Act of 1973, as amended	Provides for the conservation of threatened and endangered species of fish, wildlife, and plants by Federal action and by encouraging the establishment of State programs. It provides for the determination and listing of threatened and endangered species and the designation of critical habitats. Section 7 requires refuge managers to perform internal consultation before initiating projects that affect or may affect endangered species.
Environmental Education Act of 1990	Established the Office of Environmental Education within the Environmental Protection Agency to develop and administer a Federal environmental education program in consultation with other Federal natural resource management agencies, including the Fish and Wildlife Service.
Food Security Act of 1985, as amended (Farm Bill)	Contains several provisions that contribute to wetland conservation. The Swampbuster provisions state that farmers who convert wetlands for the purpose of planting after enactment of the law are ineligible for most farm program subsidies. It also established the Wetland Reserve Program to restore and protect wetlands through easements and restoration of the functions and values of wetlands on such easement areas.
Farmland Protection Policy Act of 1981, as amended	Minimizes the extent to which Federal programs contribute to the unnecessary conversion of farmland to nonagricultural uses. Federal programs include construction projects and the management of Federal lands.
Federal Advisory Committee Act (1972), as amended	Governs the establishment of and procedures for committees that provide advice to the Federal Government. Advisory committees may be established only if they will serve a necessary, non-duplicative function. Committees must be strictly advisory unless otherwise specified and meetings must be open to the public.

Federal Coal Leasing Amendment Act of 1976	Provided that nothing in the Mining Act, the Mineral Leasing Act, or the Mineral Leasing Act for Acquired Lands authorized mining coal on refuges.
Federal-Aid Highways Act of 1968	Established requirements for approval of Federal highways through wildlife refuges and other designated areas to preserve the natural beauty of such areas. The Secretary of Transportation is directed to consult with the Secretary of the Interior and other Federal agencies before approving any program or project requiring the use of land under their jurisdiction.
Federal Noxious Weed Act of 1990, as amended	The Secretary of Agriculture was given the authority to designate plants as noxious weeds and to cooperate with other Federal, State and local agencies, farmers' associations, and private individuals in measures to control, eradicate, prevent, or retard the spread of such weeds. The Act requires each Federal land-managing agency, including the Fish and Wildlife Service, to designate an office or person to coordinate a program to control such plants on the agency's land and implement cooperative agreements with the States, including integrated management systems to control undesirable plants.
Fish and Wildlife Act of 1956	Establishes a comprehensive national fish, shellfish, and wildlife resources policy with emphasis on the commercial fishing industry, but also includes the inherent right of every citizen and resident to fish for pleasure, enjoyment, and betterment, and to maintain and increase public opportunities for recreational use of fish and wildlife resources. Among other things, it authorizes the Secretary of the Interior to take such steps as may be required for the development, advancement, management, conservation, and protection of fish and wildlife resources, including, but not limited to, research, development of existing facilities, and acquisition by purchase or exchange of land and water or interests therein.
Fish and Wildlife Conservation Act of 1980, as amended	Requires the Service to monitor non-gamebird species, identify species of management concern, and implement conservation measures to preclude the need for listing under the Endangered Species Act.
Fish and Wildlife Coordination Act of 1958	Promotes equal consideration and coordination of wildlife conservation with other water resource development programs by requiring consultation with the Fish and Wildlife Service and the State fish and wildlife agencies where the "waters of a stream or other body of water are proposed or authorized, permitted or licensed to be impounded, diverted...or otherwise controlled or modified" by any agency under Federal permit or license.
Improvement Act of 1978	Passed to improve the administration of fish and wildlife programs and amends several earlier laws, including the Refuge Recreation Act, the National Wildlife Refuge Administration Act, and the Fish and Wildlife Act of 1956. It authorizes the Secretary to accept gifts and bequests of real and personal property on behalf of the United States. It also authorizes the use of volunteers on Service projects and appropriations to carry out volunteer programs.

Freedom of Information Act, 1966	Requires all Federal agencies to make available to the public for inspection and copying administrative staff manuals and staff instructions, official, published and unpublished policy statements, final orders deciding case adjudication, and other documents. Special exemptions have been reserved for nine categories of privileged material. The Act requires the party seeking the information to pay reasonable search and duplication costs. Section 15c of the Act prohibits issuing geothermal leases on virtually all Service-administrative lands.
Lacey Act of 1970, as amended	Designed to help states protect their native game animals and to safeguard U.S. crop production from harmful foreign species. This Act prohibits interstate and international transport and commerce of fish, wildlife, or plants taken in violation of domestic or foreign laws.
Land and Water Conservation Fund Act of 1948	Provides funding through receipts from the sale of surplus Federal land, appropriations from oil and gas receipts from the outer continental shelf, and other sources for land acquisition under several authorities. Appropriations from the fund may be used for matching grants to states for outdoor recreation projects and for land acquisition by various federal agencies including the Fish and Wildlife Service.
Migratory Bird Conservation Act of 1929	Established a Migratory Bird Conservation Commission to approve areas recommended by the Secretary of the Interior for acquisition with Migratory Bird Conservation Funds. The role of the Commission was expanded by the North American Wetland Conservation Act to include approving wetlands acquisition, restoration, and enhancement proposals recommended by the North American Wetlands Conservation Council.
Migratory Bird Hunting and Conservation Stamp Act of 1934	Also commonly referred to as the "Duck Stamp Act" it requires waterfowl hunters 16 years of age or older to possess a valid Federal hunting stamp. Receipts from the sale of the stamp are deposited into the Migratory Bird Conservation Fund for the acquisition of migratory bird refuges.
Migratory Bird Treaty Act of 1918, as amended	Implements various treaties and conventions between the U.S. and Canada, Japan, Mexico and the former Soviet Union for the protection of migratory birds. Except as allowed by special regulations, this Act makes it unlawful to pursue, hunt, kill, capture, possess, buy, sell, purchase, barter, export, or import any migratory bird, part, nest, egg or product.
Mineral Leasing Act for Acquired Lands (1947), as amended	Authorizes and governs mineral leasing on acquired public lands.
Minerals Leasing Act of 1920, as amended	Authorizes and governs leasing of public lands for development of deposits of coal, oil, gas and other hydrocarbons, sulphur, phosphate, potassium, and sodium. Section 185 of this title contains provisions relating to granting rights-of-way over Federal lands for pipelines.
Mining Act of 1872, as amended	Authorizes and governs prospecting and mining for the so-called "hardrock" minerals (such as gold and silver) on public lands.

National and Community Service Act of 1990	Authorizes several programs to engage citizens of the U.S. in full- and/or part-time projects designed to combat illiteracy and poverty, provide job skills, enhance educational skills, and fulfill environmental needs. Among other things, this law establishes the American Conservation and Youth Service Corps to engage young adults in approved human and natural resource projects, which will benefit the public or are carried out on Federal or Indian lands.
National Environmental Policy Act of 1969	Requires analysis, public comment, and reporting for environmental impacts of Federal actions. It stipulates the factors to be considered in environmental impact statements, and requires that Federal agencies employ an interdisciplinary approach in related decision-making and develop means to ensure that unqualified environmental values are given appropriate consideration, along with economic and technical considerations.
National Historic Preservation Act of 1966, as amended	Established a National Register of Historic Places and a program of matching grants for preservation of significant historical features. Federal agencies are directed to take into account the effects of their actions on items or sites listed or eligible for listing in the National Register.
National Trails System Act (1968), as amended	Established the National Trails System to protect the recreational, scenic and historic values of some important trails. National Recreation Trails may be established by the Secretaries of Interior or Agriculture on land wholly or partly within their jurisdiction, with the consent of the involved State(s), and other land managing agencies, if any. National Scenic and National Historic Trails may only be designated by an Act of Congress. Several National Trails cross units of the National Wildlife Refuge System.
National Wildlife Refuge System Administration Act of 1966	Prior to 1966, there was no single Federal law that governed the administration of the various wildlife refuges that had been established. This Act defines the National Wildlife Refuge System and authorizes the Secretary of the Interior to permit any use of an area provided such use is compatible with the major purposes(s) for which the area was established.
National Wildlife Refuge System Improvement Act of 1997	Amends the National Wildlife Refuge System Administration Act of 1966. This Act defines the mission of the National Wildlife Refuge System, establishes the legitimacy and appropriateness of six priority wildlife-dependent public uses, establishes a formal process for determining "compatible uses" of System lands, identifies the Secretary of the Interior as responsible for managing and protecting the System, and requires the development of a comprehensive conservation plan for all refuges outside of Alaska.
Native American Graves Protection and Repatriation Act of 1990	Requires Federal agencies and museums to inventory, determine ownership of, and repatriate certain cultural items and human remains under their control or possession. The Act also addresses the repatriation of cultural items inadvertently discovered by construction activities on lands managed by the agency.
Neotropical Migratory Bird Conservation Act of 2000	Establishes a matching grants program to fund projects that promote the conservation of neotropical migratory birds in the United States, Latin America, and the Caribbean.

North American Wetlands Conservation Act of 1989	Provides funding and administrative direction for implementation of the North American Waterfowl Management Plan and the Tripartite Agreement on wetlands between Canada, U.S., and Mexico. North American Wetlands Conservation Council is created to recommend projects to be funded under the Act to the Migratory Bird Conservation Commission. Available funds may be expended for up to 50 percent of the United States share cost of wetlands conservation projects in Canada, Mexico, or the United States (or 100 percent of the cost of projects on Federal lands).
Refuge Recreation Act of 1962, as amended	Authorizes the Secretary of the Interior to administer refuges, hatcheries, and other conservation areas for recreational use, when such uses do not interfere with the area's primary purposes. It authorizes construction and maintenance of recreational facilities and the acquisition of land for incidental fish and wildlife-dependent recreational development or protection of natural resources. It also authorizes the charging of fees for public uses.
Partnerships for Wildlife Act of 1992	Establishes a Wildlife Conservation and Appreciation Fund, to receive appropriated funds and donations from the National Fish and Wildlife Foundation and other private sources to assist the State fish and game agencies in carrying out their responsibilities for conservation of non-game species. The funding formula is no more that 1/3 Federal funds, at least 1/3 Foundation funds, and at least 1/3 State funds.
Refuge Revenue Sharing Act of 1935, as amended	Provided for payments to counties in lieu of taxes from areas administered by the Fish and Wildlife Service. Counties are required to pass payments along to other units of local government within the county, which suffer losses in tax revenues due to the establishment of Service areas.
Rehabilitation Act of 1973	Requires nondiscrimination in the employment practices of Federal agencies of the executive branch and contractors. It also requires all federally assisted programs, services, and activities to be available to people with disabilities.
Rivers and Harbors Appropriations Act of 1899, as amended	Requires authorization by the U.S. Army Corps of Engineers prior to any work in, on, over, or under a navigable water of the United States. The Fish and Wildlife Coordination Act provides authority for the Service to review and comment on the effects on fish and wildlife activities proposed to be undertaken or permitted by the Corps of Engineers. Service concerns include contaminated sediments associated with dredge or fill projects in navigable waters.
Sikes Act (1960), as amended	Provides for the cooperation by the Departments of Interior and Defense with State agencies in planning, development, and maintenance of fish and wildlife resources and outdoor recreation facilities on military reservations throughout the U.S. It requires the Secretary of each military department to use trained professionals to manage the wildlife and fishery resource under his jurisdiction, and requires Federal and State fish and wildlife agencies be given priority in management of fish and wildlife activities on military reservations.

Transfer of Certain Real Property for Wildlife Conservation Purposes Act of 1948	Provides, upon determination by the Administrator of the General Services Administration, that real property no longer needed by a Federal agency can be transferred, without reimbursement, to the Secretary of the Interior if the land has particular value for migratory birds, or to a State agency for other wildlife conservation purposes.
Transportation Equity Act for the 21st Century (1998)	Established the Refuge Roads Program, requires transportation planning that includes public involvement, and provides funding for approved public use roads and trails and associated parking lots, comfort stations and bicycle/pedestrian facilities.
Uniform Relocation and Assistance and Real Property Acquisition Policies Act (1970), as amended	Provides for uniform and equitable treatment of persons who sell their homes, businesses, or farms to the Service. The Act requires that any purchase offer be no less than the fair market value of the property.
Water Resources Planning Act of 1965	Established Water Resources Council to be composed of Cabinet representatives, including the Secretary of the Interior. The Council reviews river basin plans with respect to agricultural, urban, energy, industrial, recreational and fish and wildlife needs. The Act also established a grant program to assist States in participating in the development of related comprehensive water and land use plans.
Wild and Scenic Rivers Act of 1968, as amended	Selects certain rivers of the nation possessing remarkable scenic, recreational, geologic, fish and wildlife, historic, cultural, or other similar values; preserves them in a free-flowing condition; and protects their local environments.
Wilderness Act of 1964, as amended	Directs the Secretary of the Interior to review every roadless area of 5,000 acres or more and every roadless island regardless of size within the National Wildlife Refuge System and to recommend suitability of each such area as wilderness. The Act permits certain activities within designated Wilderness Areas that do not alter natural processes. Wilderness values are preserved through a "minimum tool" management approach, which requires refuge managers to use the least intrusive methods, equipment, and facilities necessary for administering the areas.

EXECUTIVE ORDERS	DESCRIPTIONS
EO 11593, Protection and Enhancement of the Cultural Environment (1971)	States that if the Service proposes any development activities that may affect the archaeological or historic sites, the Service will consult with Federal and State Historic Preservation Officers to comply with Section 106 of the National Historic Preservation Act of 1966, as amended.
EO 11644, Use of Off-road Vehicles on Public Land (1972)	Established policies and procedures to ensure that the use of off-road vehicles on public lands will be controlled and directed so as to protect the resources of those lands, to promote the safety of all users of those lands, and to minimize conflicts among the various uses of those lands.
EO 11988, Floodplain Management (1977)	The purpose of this Executive Order is to prevent Federal agencies from contributing to the "adverse impacts associated with occupancy and modification of floodplains" and the "direct or indirect support of floodplain development." In the course of fulfilling their respective authorities, Federal agencies "shall take action to reduce the risk of flood loss, to minimize the impact of floods on human safety, health and welfare, and to restore and preserve the natural and beneficial values served by floodplains.
EO 11989 (1977), Amends Section 2 of EO 11644	Directs agencies to close areas that are negatively impacted by off-road vehicles.
EO 11990, Protection of Wetlands (1977)	Directs Federal agencies are directed to provide leadership and take action to minimize the destruction, loss of degradation of wetlands, and to preserve and enhance the natural and beneficial values of wetlands.
EO 12372, Intergovernmental Review of Federal Programs (1982)	Seeks to foster intergovernmental partnerships by requiring Federal agencies to use the State process to determine and address concerns of State and local elected officials with proposed Federal assistance and development programs.
EO 12898, Environmental Justice (1994)	Requires Federal agencies to identify and address disproportionately high and adverse effects of its programs, policies, and activities on minority and low-income populations.

EXECUTIVE ORDERS	DESCRIPTIONS
EO 12906, Coordinating Geographical Data Acquisition and Access (1994), Amended by EO 13286 (2003). Amendment of EO's & other actions in connection w/ transfer of certain functions to Secretary of DHS.	Recommended that the executive branch develop, in cooperation with State, local, and Tribal governments, and the private sector, a coordinated National Spatial Data Infrastructure to support public and private sector applications of geospatial data. Of particular importance to CCP planning is the National Vegetation Classification System (NVCS), which is the adopted standard for vegetation mapping. Using NVCS facilitates the compilation of regional and national summaries, which in turn, can provide an ecosystem context for individual refuges.
EO 12962, Recreational Fisheries (1995)	Directs Federal agencies to improve the quantity, function, sustainable productivity, and distribution of U.S. aquatic resources for increased recreational fishing opportunities in cooperation with States and Tribes.
EO 13007, Native American Religious Practices (1996)	Provides for access to, and ceremonial use of, Indian sacred sites on Federal lands used by Indian religious practitioners and direction to avoid adversely affecting the physical integrity of such sites.
EO 13061, Federal Support of Community Efforts Along American Heritage Rivers (1997)	Established the American Heritage Rivers initiative for the purpose of natural resource and environmental protection, economic revitalization, and historic and cultural preservation. The Act directs Federal agencies to preserve, protect, and restore rivers and their associated resources important to our history, culture, and natural heritage.
EO 13084, Consultation and Coordination With Indian Tribal Governments (2000)	Provides a mechanism for establishing regular and meaningful consultation and collaboration with tribal officials in the development of Federal policies that have tribal implications.
EO 13112, Invasive Species (1999)	Directs Federal agencies to prevent the introduction of invasive species, detect and respond rapidly to and control populations of such species in a cost effective and environmentally sound manner, accurately monitor invasive species, provide for restoration of native species and habitat conditions, conduct research to prevent introductions and to control invasive species, and promote public education on invasive species and the means to address them. This EO replaces and rescinds EO 11987, Exotic Organisms (1977).

EXECUTIVE ORDERS	DESCRIPTIONS
EO 13186, Responsibilities of Federal Agencies to Protect Migratory Birds. (2001)	Instructs Federal agencies to conserve migratory birds by several means, including the incorporation of strategies and recommendations found in Partners in Flight Bird Conservation plans, the North American Waterfowl Plan, the North American Waterbird Conservation Plan, and the United States Shorebird Conservation Plan, into agency management plans and guidance documents.

Appendix D. Public Involvement

SUMMARY OF PUBLIC INVOLVEMENT PROCESS

Preparation for the Draft CCP development process usually begins with a Biological Review and a Public Use Review. Since the planning team members were the most knowledgeable persons for the biological resources of the refuge and since the refuge is currently closed to all public use, neither of these reviews were conducted.

On October 28, 2005, the Logan Cave Planning Team was formed to identify issues and concerns regarding the refuge and its wildlife, habitats, and management. This team consisted of key members from Holla Bend NWR, Ozark Plateau NWR, individuals from the Arkansas Game and Fish Commission, The Nature Conservancy of Arkansas, and the Service's Ecological Services Conway, Arkansas, Field Office. Members from Holla Bend NWR staff included: the project leader and assistant manager. Ozark Plateau NWR staff included the refuge manager. Ecological Services also provided a Karst biologist. Outside agency participants included: TNC Ozark Karst Program biologist, and a state non-game wildlife biologist. The planning team held its initial meeting on October 18, 2005, to develop a vision, outline management goals, and provide direction for organizing public meetings.

A Draft CCP mailing list was developed for Logan Cave NWR that consisted of individuals from the general public, landowners, state agencies, organizations, governments, and other interested agencies. In March 2006, announcements of the first public scoping meeting were included in local (Benton County) newspapers and one state-wide newspaper.

On April 20, 2006, a public scoping meeting was conducted at the Logan Community Building to obtain information and concerns from the public in the community surrounding the refuge. A total of 30 people attended the meeting.

Comment sheets and maps of the refuge and recharge zone were available at the meeting. A brief presentation on the planning and environmental compliance processes was given by the project leader for Logan Cave NWR. The assistant refuge manager provided the audience with an overview of the refuge and wildlife management activities. Following the formal presentations, attendees were given the opportunity to express their concerns, thoughts, and ideas on refuge management.

The planning team met again on June 21, 2006, to finalize the vision statement for the refuge and develop refuge goals, strategies and projects to be included in the Draft CCP.

The team meetings and the public scoping meeting provided a list of priority issues that participants believed needed to be addressed in the Draft CCP. A list of alternatives to address identified issues was developed. The proposed action formed the basis for development of objectives and strategies that are expected to achieve the goals identified by the planning team. This process ensured that the most important issues would be resolved or given priority over the life of the CCP. The summaries of the priority issues, along with some discussion on their impacts to the resources, are located in Chapter III.

SUMMARY OF DRAFT CCP PUBLIC COMMENTS

Public involvement in the development of the CCP for Logan Cave National Wildlife Refuge, Benton County, Arkansas, was sought throughout the planning process. The CCP will guide management direction of the refuge over the next 15 years.

The issues and alternatives generated from the scoping meeting, coupled with the input of the planning team, are summarized in Chapter III.

Approximately 120 copies of the Draft CCP/EA were made available for public review, beginning January 25, 2008, and ending February 25, 2008. A flyer, which announced the date of the comment period and the date and location of the public meeting to discuss the Draft CCP/EA, was mailed along with the plans. A public meeting was held on February 12, 2008, at 6:00 p.m., at the Logan Community Center. Fifteen individuals were in attendance at the meeting. Eight respondents consisting of the Service; the State Clearinghouse of Arkansas, Department of Finance and Administration; the Ozark Underground Laboratory, Inc.; Natural Resources Conservation Service; the Arkansas Natural Heritage Commission; and local citizens submitted written comments by mail or email. Draft CCP/EA comments and the Service response to those comments are summarized below.

DRAFT PLAN COMMENTS AND SERVICE RESPONSES

General

Two respondents provided general editorial comments.

Service Response: The Service will incorporate these changes where appropriate.

One respondent believed that none of the alternatives would have an adverse affect on Prime Farmland or Farmland of Statewide Importance in the area. Alternatives 1 and 3 would enhance and protect the natural resources in the area. Alternative 3 would best preserve the natural resources in the area.

One respondent mentioned that the Federal Cave Resource Protection Act might back us up on some of the things we want to do.

Service Response: It is undetermined if Logan Cave has been nominated as a significant cave under the 1988 Federal Cave Resources Protection Act (Public Law 100-691). The Federal Cave Resources Protection Act recognizes significant caves and establishes a formal program for federal land managers to identify, list, manage, and protect the significant caves on their lands. The Service will add a strategy under the Resource Protection Goal to determine designation of Logan Cave.

Fish and Wildlife Population Management

One respondent states that Logan Cave historically provided habitat for one other listed species, the Indiana bat (*Myotis sodalis*), in addition to the three species consulted upon. Additionally, the site is known to support at least two species of state conservation concern: grotto salamander (*Eurycea spelaeus*); and a cave obligate millipede (*Trigenotyla parca*).

Service Response: The Service will ensure the state designation and cooperative conservation of these species as cited throughout the CCP.

Habitat Management

One respondent believes the Service should use the word karst to describe geologic features of Logan Cave.

Service Response: The Service agrees and uses the word "karst" throughout the document where appropriate.

Resource Protection

One respondent believes water quality studies could be strengthened by focusing on parameters likely to be associated with Confined Animal Feeding Operations (CAFOs) and land application of CAFO wastes. The respondent states that these parameters will vary substantially with time and with precipitation events.

Service Response: Water testing will be ongoing and continuous water testing sites will be maintained. Testing will be specific enough to determine confined or residential contaminants.

One respondent believes the Service should use best management practices when disturbing the soils, such as the Clarksville and Noark soils which can be quite erodible when disturbed.

Service Response: The Service agrees and will use best management practices in any management action, especially in research areas.

One respondent states that Logan Cave is actually in Bailey's Ozark Ecoregion and the Service's Ozark Ecosystem even though some maps show it in the Ark/Red Ecosystem.

Service Response: The administrative boundary of Logan Cave is located in the Arkansas/Red River Ecosystem. The Service does actively participate in the Ozark Ecosystem activities and will strive to further coordinate within both ecosystems.

Visitor Services

One respondent believes enforcement and fines for hunting trespassing should be issued.

Service Response: There is no public access to site and state and federal law enforcement protects this resource.

Two respondents believe hiring a public use specialist stationed near Logan Cave to develop environmental education programs would be better than locating the position at the Holla Bend NWR Headquarters. One respondent suggests contracting with a person, company, or organization located close to Logan Cave to develop the visitor services' programs for the refuge. One respondent would like the Service to develop a Friends of Logan Cave group with the purpose of establishing a volunteer corps to provide visitor services for the refuge.

Service Response: Although the Service believes a refuge manager position is the highest priority, these suggestions will be considered in order to coordinate conservation efforts. The Service will also change Objective 1 under the Visitor Services' Goal to include looking into these options.

One respondent believes mentioning the cavers, local grottos, and National Speleological Society (NSS) might help us if we need help from them in the future. The respondent further indicates that the Service does have a National Memorandum of Understanding with the NSS.

Service Response: The Service agrees and will change the text in the document to include additional partnerships and coordinated management activities.

Refuge Administration

The Department of Arkansas Heritage offers technical assistance to refuge staff to assist in conducting work related to rare species and natural communities on the area. Ozark Plateau NWR is close and willing to help where we can. Also Ozark Cavefish NWR and Pilot Knob NWR are federally listed cave species refuges not too far away in Missouri managed by Mingo NWR. It might help to mention coordination in managing these areas across state and FWS regional boundaries.

Service Response: The Service appreciates the assistance and will strive to build strong cooperative partnerships.

Appendix E. Appropriate Use Determinations

Logan Cave National Wildlife Refuge Appropriate Use Determinations

An appropriate use determination is the initial decision process a refuge manager follows when first considering whether or not to allow a proposed use on a refuge. The refuge manager must find that a use is appropriate before undertaking a compatibility review of the use. This process clarifies and expands on the compatibility determination process by describing when refuge managers should deny a proposed use without determining compatibility. If a proposed use is not appropriate, it will not be allowed and a compatibility determination will not be undertaken.

Except for the uses noted below, the refuge manager must decide if a new or existing use is an appropriate refuge use. If an existing use is not appropriate, the refuge manager will eliminate or modify the use as expeditiously as practicable. If a new use is not appropriate, the refuge manager will deny the use without determining compatibility. Uses that have been administratively determined to be appropriate are:

- Six wildlife-dependent recreational uses - As defined by the National Wildlife Refuge System Improvement Act of 1997, the six wildlife-dependent recreational uses (hunting, fishing, wildlife observation, wildlife photography, and environmental education and interpretation) are determined to be appropriate. However, the refuge manager must still determine if these uses are compatible.

- Take of fish and wildlife under state regulations - States have regulations concerning take of wildlife that includes hunting, fishing, and trapping. The Service considers take of wildlife under such regulations appropriate. However, the refuge manager must determine if the activity is compatible before allowing it on a refuge.

Statutory Authorities for this policy:

National Wildlife Refuge System Administration Act of 1966, as amended by the National Wildlife Refuge System Improvement Act of 1997, 16 U.S.C. §668dd-668ee. This law provides the authority for establishing policies and regulations governing refuge uses, including the authority to prohibit certain harmful activities. The Act does not authorize any particular use, but rather authorizes the Secretary of the Interior to allow uses only when they are compatible and "under such regulations as he may prescribe." This law specifically identifies certain public uses that, when compatible, are legitimate and appropriate uses within the Refuge System. The law states ". . . it is the policy of the United States that . . .compatible wildlife-dependent recreation is a legitimate and appropriate general public use of the System . . .compatible wildlife-dependent recreational uses are the priority general public uses of the System and shall receive priority consideration in refuge planning and management; and . . . when the Secretary determines that a proposed wildlife-dependent recreational use is a compatible use within a refuge, that activity should be facilitated . . . the Secretary shall . . . ensure that priority general public uses of the System receive enhanced consideration over other general public uses in planning and management within the System . . . ." The law also states "in administering the System, the Secretary is authorized to take the following actions: . . . issue regulations to carry out this Act." This policy implements the standards set in the Act by providing enhanced consideration of priority general public uses and ensuring other public uses do not interfere with our ability to provide quality, wildlife-dependent recreational uses.

Refuge Recreation Act of 1962, 16 U.S.C. 460k. The Act authorizes the Secretary of the Interior to administer refuges, hatcheries, and other conservation areas for recreational use, when such uses do not interfere with the area's primary purposes. It authorizes construction and maintenance of recreational facilities and the acquisition of land for incidental fish and wildlife oriented recreational development or protection of natural resources. It also authorizes the charging of fees for public uses.

Other Statutes that Establish Refuges, including the Alaska National Interest Lands Conservation Act of 1980 (ANILCA) (16 U.S.C. §410hh - 410hh-5, 460 mm - 460mm-4, 539-539e, and 3101 - 3233; 43 U.S.C. 1631 et seq.).

Executive Orders. The Service must comply with Executive Order 11644 when allowing use of off-highway vehicles on refuges. This order requires the Service to designate areas as open or closed to off-highway vehicles in order to protect refuge resources, promote safety, and minimize conflict among the various refuge users; monitor the effects of these uses once they are allowed; and amend or rescind any area designation as necessary based on the information gathered. Furthermore, Executive Order 11989 requires the Service to close areas to off-highway vehicles when it is determined that the use causes or will cause considerable adverse effects on the soil, vegetation, wildlife, habitat, or cultural or historic resources. Statutes, such as ANILCA, take precedence over executive orders.

Definitions:

Appropriate Use
A proposed or existing use on a refuge that meets at least one of the following four conditions.

1) The use is a wildlife-dependent recreational use as identified in the Improvement Act.
2) The use contributes to fulfilling the refuge purpose(s), the Refuge System mission, or goals or objectives described in a refuge management plan approved after October 9, 1997, the date the Improvement Act was signed into law.
3) The use involves the take of fish and wildlife under state regulations.
4) The use has been found to be appropriate as specified in section 1.11.

Native American. American Indians in the conterminous United States and Alaska Natives (including Aleuts, Eskimos, and Indians) who are members of federally recognized tribes.

Priority General Public Use. A compatible wildlife-dependent recreational use of a refuge involving hunting, fishing, wildlife observation, wildlife photography, and environmental education and interpretation.

Quality. The criteria used to determine a quality recreational experience include:

- Promotes safety of participants, other visitors, and facilities.
- Promotes compliance with applicable laws and regulations and responsible behavior.
- Minimizes or eliminates conflicts with fish and wildlife population or habitat goals or objectives in a plan approved after 1997.
- Minimizes or eliminates conflicts with other compatible wildlife-dependent recreation.
- Minimizes conflicts with neighboring landowners.
- Promotes accessibility and availability to a broad spectrum of the American people.
- Promotes resource stewardship and conservation.

- Promotes public understanding and increases public appreciation of America's natural resources and the Service's role in managing and protecting these resources.
- Provides reliable/reasonable opportunities to experience wildlife.
- Uses facilities that are accessible and blend into the natural setting.
- Uses visitor satisfaction to help define and evaluate programs.

Wildlife-Dependent Recreational Use. As defined by the Improvement Act, a use of a refuge involving hunting, fishing, wildlife observation, wildlife photography, and environmental education and interpretation.

FINDING OF APPROPRIATENESS OF A REFUGE USE

Refuge Name: ___Logan Cave National Wildlife Refuge___

Use: ___Research and Monitoring___

This form is not required for wildlife-dependent recreational uses, take regulated by the State, or uses already described in a refuge CCP or step-down management plan approved after October 9, 1997.

Decision Criteria:	YES	NO
(a) Do we have jurisdiction over the use?	X	
(b) Does the use comply with applicable laws and regulations (Federal, State, tribal, and local)?	X	
(c) Is the use consistent with applicable executive orders and Department and Service policies?	X	
(d) Is the use consistent with public safety?	X	
(e) Is the use consistent with goals and objectives in an approved management plan or other document?	X	
(f) Has an earlier documented analysis not denied the use or is this the first time the use has been proposed?		X
(g) Is the use manageable within available budget and staff?	X	
(h) Will this be manageable in the future within existing resources?		X
(i) Does the use contribute to the public's understanding and appreciation of the refuge's natural or cultural resources, or is the use beneficial to the refuge's natural or cultural resources?	X	
(j) Can the use be accommodated without impairing existing wildlife-dependent recreational uses or reducing the potential to provide quality (see section 1.6D, 603 FW 1, for description), compatible, wildlife-dependent recreation into the future?	X	

Where we do not have jurisdiction over the use ["no" to (a)], there is no need to evaluate it further as we cannot control the use. Uses that are illegal, inconsistent with existing policy, or unsafe ["no" to (b), (c), or (d)] may not be found appropriate. If the answer is "no" to any of the other questions above, we will **generally** not allow the use.

If indicated, the refuge manager has consulted with State fish and wildlife agencies.   **Yes _X_ No ___**

When the refuge manager finds the use appropriate based on sound professional judgment, the refuge manager must justify the use in writing on an attached sheet and obtain the refuge supervisor's concurrence.

Based on an overall assessment of these factors, my summary conclusion is that the proposed use is:

Not Appropriate _____   Appropriate __X__

Refuge Manager: _____   Date: __7/3/2008__

If found to be **Not Appropriate**, the refuge supervisor does not need to sign concurrence if the use is a new use. If an existing use is found **Not Appropriate** outside the CCP process, the refuge supervisor must sign concurrence. If found to be **Appropriate**, the refuge supervisor must sign concurrence.

Refuge Supervisor: _____ Acting sign   Date: __7/11/08__

A compatibility determination is required before the use may be allowed.

Appendix F. Compatibility Determinations

Logan Cave National Wildlife Refuge Compatibility Determination

Uses: Refuge Resource Research and Monitoring and Environmental Education and Interpretation were found to be appropriate and evaluated to determine their compatibility with the mission of the Refuge System and the purposes of the refuge.

Refuge Name: Logan Cave National Wildlife Refuge.

Date Established: March 14, 1989.

Establishing and Acquisition Authority(ies): The Logan Cave National Wildlife Refuge, located in Benton County, Arkansas, was established on March 14, 1989, by the Endangered Species Act of 1973.

Refuge Purpose: For lands acquired under the Endangered Species Act (16 U.S.C., Section 1534), the purpose of the acquisition is "…..to conserve fish or wildlife which are listed as endangered species or threatened species….. "

National Wildlife Refuge System Mission:

The mission of the Refuge System, as defined by the National Wildlife Refuge System Improvement Act of 1997, is:

> *… to administer a national network of lands and waters for the conservation, management, and where appropriate, restoration of the fish, wildlife and plant resources and their habitats within the United States for the benefit of present and future generations of Americans.*

Other Applicable Laws, Regulations, and Policies:

Antiquities Act of 1906 (34 Stat. 225)
Migratory Bird Treaty Act of 1918 (15 U.S.C. 703-711; 40 Stat. 755)
Migratory Bird Conservation Act of 1929 (16 U.S.C. 715r; 45 Stat. 1222)
Migratory Bird Hunting Stamp Act of 1934 (16 U.S.C. 718-178h; 48 Stat. 451)
Criminal Code Provisions of 1940 (18 U.S.C. 41)
Bald and Golden Eagle Protection Act (16 U.S.C. 668-668d; 54 Stat. 250)
Refuge Trespass Act of June 25, 1948 (18 U.S.C. 41; 62 Stat. 686)
Fish and Wildlife Act of 1956 (16 U.S.C. 742a-742j; 70 Stat.1119)
Refuge Recreation Act of 1962 (16 U.S.C. 460k-460k-4; 76 Stat. 653)
Wilderness Act (16 U.S.C. 1131; 78 Stat. 890)
Land and Water Conservation Fund Act of 1965
National Historic Preservation Act of 1966, as amended (16 U.S.C. 470, et seq.; 80 Stat. 915)
National Wildlife Refuge System Administration Act of 1966 (16 U.S.C. 668dd, 668ee; 80 Stat. 927)
National Environmental Policy Act of 1969, NEPA (42 U.S.C. 4321, et seq; 83 Stat. 852)
Use of Off-Road Vehicles on Public Lands (Executive Order 11644, as amended by Executive Order 10989)
Endangered Species Act of 1973 (16 U.S.C. 1531 et seq; 87 Stat. 884)
Refuge Revenue Sharing Act of 1935, as amended in 1978 (16 U.S.C. 715s; 92 Stat. 1319)

National Wildlife Refuge Regulations for the Most Recent Fiscal Year (50 CFR Subchapter C; 43 CFR 3101.3-3)

Emergency Wetlands Resources Act of 1986 (S.B. 740)

North American Wetlands Conservation Act of 1990

Food Security Act (Farm Bill) of 1990 as amended (HR 2100)

The Property Clause of the U.S. Constitution Article IV 3, Clause 2

The Commerce Clause of the U.S. Constitution Article 1, Section 8

The National Wildlife Refuge System Improvement Act of 1997 (Public Law 105-57, USC668dd)

Executive Order 12996, Management and General Public Use of the National Wildlife Refuge System. March 25, 1996

Title 50, Code of Federal Regulations, Parts 25-33

Archaeological Resources Protection Act of 1979

Native American Graves Protection and Repatriation Act of 1990

Compatibility determinations for each description listed were considered separately. Although for brevity, the preceding sections from "Uses" through "Other Applicable Laws, Regulations and Policies" and the succeeding sections, "Literature Cited," "Public Review," and the "Approval of Compatibility Determinations" are only written once within the CCP, they are part of each descriptive use and become part of that compatibility determination if considered outside of the CCP.

Description of Use: Refuge Resource Research and Monitoring.

This use will allow university students, professors, and governmental scientists to access the cave environment to conduct both short-term and long-term research projects. Allowing this research will result in better knowledge of our cave resources and improved techniques to manage, monitor, and protect these resources. The refuge will support research of two endangered species, the gray bat and Benton cave crayfish, and one threatened species, the Ozark cavefish. A strong effort will be made to continue and to expand partnerships with the University of Arkansas on researching these rare and unique species.

Availability of Resources: No additional staff or monetary resources are needed to allow this use. Existing staff can administer permits and monitor use as part of routine management duties.

Anticipated Impacts of the Use: As long as sound scientific methods are used to conduct research, no significant negative impacts should occur from scientific studies on the refuge. The knowledge gained would provide information to improve management techniques and better understand the needs of these trust resource species. Impacts such as trampling vegetation and temporary disturbance to wildlife will occur, but will be minimal.

Public Review and Comment: This compatibility determination was part of the Draft Comprehensive Conservation Plan and Environmental Assessment (Draft CCP/EA), which was announced in the *Federal Register* (73 FR 4615) and made available for public comment from January 25, 2008, until February 25, 2008. Copies of the Draft CCP/EA were available at refuge headquarters and area locations; more than 120 copies were distributed to local landowners; the public; and local, state, and federal agencies. A public meeting was also held on February 12, 2008, near Logan Cave.

Determination (check one below):

_____ Use is Not Compatible

__X__ Use is Compatible with Following Stipulations

Stipulations Necessary to Ensure Compatibility: Each request for use of the refuge for research would be examined on its individual merit. If sound scientific methods are being proposed and refuge staff determines that requested research can be conducted without significantly affecting wildlife resources, the use will be allowed. The researcher will be issued a special use permit stating the conditions that must be followed. Progress will be monitored and researchers will be required to submit annual progress reports and copies of all publications derived from the research. Since the cave is home to a large maternity colony of gray bats, any research will be done in the winter months so there will be no disturbance to the colony.

Justification: The benefits from scientifically sound research provide a better understanding of this very unique habitat and its species. These benefits far outweigh any short-term disturbance that might occur.

Mandatory 10-year Re-evaluation Date: _____8/8/2018_____

Description of Use: Environmental Education and Interpretation.

This use will allow limited scheduled and guided environmental education and interpretation at the refuge. Off-refuge programs will be conducted to the extent possible. Educating the public about the natural resources in their community is the best way to gain their cooperation and understanding of refuge management projects.

Availability of Resources: Current and any future refuge staff will be present for on-refuge programs. Additional staff will be needed to make this program a success.

Anticipated Impacts of the Use: No significant negative impacts will occur from environmental education. The knowledge gained by the public will allow a better understanding of the trust resource species. On-refuge programs will have impacts, such as trampling vegetation and temporary disturbance to terrestrial wildlife, but should be minimal.

Public Review and Comment: This compatibility determination was part of the Draft Comprehensive Conservation Plan and Environmental Assessment (Draft CCP/EA), which was announced in the *Federal Register* (73 FR 4615) and made available for public comment from January 25, 2008, until February 25, 2008. Copies of the Draft CCP/EA were available at refuge headquarters and area locations; more than 120 copies were distributed to local landowners; the public; and local, state, and federal agencies. A public meeting was also held on February 12, 2008, near Logan Cave.

Determination (check one below):

_____ Use is Not Compatible

__X__ Use is Compatible with Following Stipulations

Stipulations Necessary to Ensure Compatibility: On-refuge programs will be scheduled with refuge staff conducting the program. No entrance into the cave will be allowed at any time. Off-refuge programs can be administered by refuge staff or volunteers.

Justification: Environmental education and interpretation about refuge resources provides the public with a better understanding of this very unique habitat and its species. These benefits far outweigh any short-term disturbance that might occur.

Mandatory 15-year Re-evaluation Date: _____8/8/2023_____

Approval of Compatibility Determinations

The signature of approval is for all compatibility determinations considered within the Comprehensive Conservation Plan for Logan Cave National Wildlife Refuge. If one of the descriptive uses is considered for compatibility outside of the comprehensive conservation plan, the approval signature becomes part of that determination.

Refuge Manager: _____ 7/3/2008 _____
(Signature/Date)

Regional Compatibility
Coordinator: _____ 4/26/08 _____
(Signature/Date)

Refuge Supervisor: _____Richard P Ingram__ 7/23/08 ___
(Signature/Date)

Regional Chief, National
Wildlife Refuge System,
Southeast Region: _____ 7-28-08 _____
(Signature/Date)

Appendix G. Intra-Service Section 7 Biological Evaluation

Originating Person: Ben Mense
Telephone Number: 479-229-4300
E-Mail: ben_mense@fws.gov
Date: May 30, 2007

PROJECT NAME:

I.   **Service Program:**
      ___ Ecological Services
      ___ Federal Aid
      ___ Clean Vessel Act
      ___ Coastal Wetlands
      ___ Endangered Species Section 6
      ___ Partners for Fish and Wildlife
      ___ Sport Fish Restoration
      ___ Wildlife Restoration
      ___ Fisheries
      _X_ Refuges/Wildlife

II.   **State/Agency:** Arkansas/U.S. Fish and Wildlife Service

III.   **Station Name:** Logan Cave National Wildlife Refuge

IV.   **Description of Proposed Action:** Implementation of the Comprehensive Conservation Plan for Logan Cave NWR by adopting the preferred alternative of Ecosystem Emphasis, which will provide guidance, management direction, and operation plans for the next 15 years.

V.   **Pertinent Species and Habitat:**

    A.   **Include species/habitat occurrence map:** Logan Cave provides essential habitat for the endangered gray bat (*Myotis grisescens*); endangered Benton cave crayfish (*Cambarus aculabrum*); threatened Ozark Cavefish (*Amblyopsis rosae*); and historically, the endangered Indiana bat (*Myotis sodalist*).

        Adult female gray bats utilize the cave from March through August as a maternity site for raising their young. Late summer emergent counts for Logan Cave average around 20,000 bats. The gray bat is probably one of the most restricted to cave habitats of any U.S. mammal. With rare exception, it roosts in caves year-round. Because of highly specific roost and habitat requirements, fewer than 5 percent of available caves are suitable for occupation by gray bats.

Logan Cave is one of only four known habitats for the Benton cave crayfish. Cave crayfish are highly specialized for living in stable cave environments with low light and low temperatures and are unable to cope with changes in the habitats that may be induced by human activities. Logan Cave NWR has the largest known population of Benton cave crayfish in the country.

The threatened Ozark cavefish is found in several caves and springs in northwest Arkansas, southwest Missouri, and northwest Oklahoma. Logan Cave's population is the second largest known. All of the caves with cavefish contain some comparatively large source of allochthonous energy, usually bat guano or leaf litter.

Logan Cave was once used as a hibernacula site for the Indiana bat, although none have been observed for decades.

B.   Complete the following table:

SPECIES/CRITICAL HABITAT	STATUS[1]
Gray Bat (*Myotis grisescens*)	E
Indiana Bat (*Myotis sodalis*)	E
Ozark Cavefish (*Amblyopsis rosae*)	T
Benton cave crayfish (*Cambarus aculabrum*)	E

[1]*STATUS: E=endangered, T=threatened, PE=proposed endangered, PT=proposed threatened, CH=critical habitat, PCH=proposed critical habitat, C=candidate species, S/A=Similar Appearance*

VI.   Location (attach map):

A.   **Ecoregion Number and Name:** Arkansas/Red River No. 15

B.   **County and State:** Benton, Arkansas

C.   **Section, township, and range (or latitude and longitude):** Section 33, T18N, R32W.

D.   **Distance (miles) and direction to nearest town:** Twenty miles southeast to Springdale, AR

E.   Species/habitat occurrence:

Gray bat – females utilize cave during spring and summer as maternity site.

Benton cave crayfish – known to occur throughout the cave, most occurrences in upper reaches of the cave stream.

Ozark cavefish – known to occur throughout the cave, most occurrences in upper reaches of the cave stream

Indiana bat – historical use of cave as winter hibernacula, no known current use.

VII.   Determination of Effects:

A. Explanation of effects of the action on species and critical habitats in item V. B:

SPECIES/ CRITICAL HABITAT	IMPACTS TO SPECIES/CRITICAL HABITAT
Gray Bat	No negative impacts foreseen, more protection
Benton cave crayfish	No negative impacts foreseen, more protection
Ozark Cavefish	No negative impacts foreseen, more protection
Indiana Bat	No negative impacts foreseen, more protection

B.   Explanation of actions to be implemented to reduce adverse effects:

SPECIES/ CRITICAL HABITAT	ACTIONS TO MITIGATE/MINIMIZE IMPACTS
Gray Bat	Maintain protection of cave and expand protection of foraging habitats.
Benton cave crayfish	Maintain protection of cave and expand protection of groundwater within recharge area of cave stream.
Ozark Cavefish	Maintain protection of cave and expand protection of groundwater within recharge area of cave stream.
Indiana Bat	Maintain cave as potential hibernacula.

VIII. Effect Determination and Response Requested:

SPECIES/CRITICAL HABITAT	DETERMINATION[1]			REQUESTED
	NE	NA	AA	
Gray Bat		X		Concurrence
Benton cave crayfish		X		Concurrence
Ozark Cavefish		X		Concurrence
Indiana Bat		X		Concurrence

[1]*DETERMINATION/ RESPONSE REQUESTED:*
NE = no effect. This determination is appropriate when the proposed action will not directly, indirectly, or cumulatively impact, either positively or negatively, any listed, proposed, candidate species or designated/proposed critical habitat. Response Requested is optional but a "Concurrence" is recommended for a complete Administrative Record.

NA = not likely to adversely affect. This determination is appropriate when the proposed action is not likely to adversely impact any listed, proposed, candidate species or designated/proposed critical habitat or there may be beneficial effects to these resources. Response Requested
is a" Concurrence".

AA = likely to adversely affect. This determination is appropriate when the proposed action is likely to adversely impact any listed, proposed, candidate species or designated/proposed critical habitat. Response Requested for listed species is "Formal Consultation". Response requested for proposed and candidate species is "Conference".

7/3/2008

Signature (originating station)   6/1/07
    Date

Refuge Manager
Title

IX.   Reviewing Ecological Services Office Evaluation:

A. Concurrence _____   Nonconcurrence _____

B. Formal consultation required _____

C. Conference required _____

D. Informal conference required _____

E. Remarks (attach additional pages as needed):

Margaret Harney   *7/20/07*
Signature   **Date**

Acting Field Supervisor   *Arkansas Field Office*
Title   **Office**

Appendix H. Wilderness Review

Refuge planning policy requires a wilderness review as part of the comprehensive conservation planning process. The Wilderness Act of 1964 defines a wilderness area as an area of federal land that retains its primeval character and influence, without permanent improvements or human habitation, and is managed so as to preserve its natural conditions and which:

1) generally appears to have been affected primarily by the forces of nature, with the imprint of man's work substantially unnoticeable;

2) has outstanding opportunities for solitude or primitive and unconfined type of recreation;

3) has at least 5,000 contiguous roadless acres or is of sufficient size to make practicable its preservation and use in an unimpaired condition;

4) does not substantially exhibit the effects of logging, farming, grazing, or other extensive development or alteration of the landscape, or its wilderness character could be restored through appropriate management, at the time of review; and

5) may contain ecological, geological, or other features of scientific, education, scenic, or historic value.

SUMMARY OF REFUGE WILDERNESS REVIEW

The determination to recommend (or not recommend) a Wilderness Study Area to Congress for wilderness designation is made through the comprehensive conservation plan decision-making process.

The Service inventoried refuge lands within the planning area and found no areas that meet the eligibility criteria for a Wilderness Study Area as defined by the Wilderness Act. Therefore, the suitability of refuge lands for wilderness designation is not analyzed in this CCP.

Appendix I. Refuge Biota

BIRDS OBSERVED ON THE REFUGE

Great Blue Heron
Green Heron
Little Blue Heron
Canada Goose
Wood Duck
Turkey Vulture
Bald Eagle
Red-tailed Hawk
Killdeer
Great Horned Owl
Morning Dove
Yellow-billed Cuckoo
Ruby-throated Hummingbird
Belted Kingfisher
Red-headed Woodpecker
Red-bellied Woodpecker
Downy Woodpecker
Hairy Woodpecker
Northern Flicker
Pileated Woodpecker
Acadian Flycatcher
Eastern Wood-peewee
Eastern Phoebe
Great Crested Flycatcher
Barn Swallow
Chimney Swift
White-eyed Vireo
Louisiana Waterthrush
Yellow-throated Vireo
Red-eyed Vireo
Blue Jay
Fish Crow
American Crow
Carolina Chickadee
Tufted Titmouse
Carolina Wren
Winter Wren
Ruby –crowned Kinglet
Blue-gray Gnatcatcher
Eastern Bluebird
Swainson's Thrush
Hermit Thrush

Wood Thrush
American Robin
Gray Catbird
Loggerhead Shrike
Northern Mockingbird
Brown Thrasher
European Starling
Cedar Waxwing
Tennessee Warbler
Black-and-white Warbler
Northern Parula
Black-throated Green Warbler
Yellow Warbler
Yellow-rumped Warbler
Yellow-throated Warbler
American Redstart
Ovenbird
Warbling Vireo
Kentucky Warbler
Hooded Warbler
Common Yellowthroat
Yellow-breasted Chat
Summer Tanager
Eastern Towhee
Chipping Sparrow
White-breasted Nuthatch
Field Sparrow
Lincoln's Sparrow
White-crowned Sparrow
White-throated Sparrow
Dark-eyed Junco
Northern Cardinal
Rose-breasted Grosbeak
Indigo Bunting
Red-Winged Blackbird
Eastern Meadowlark
Common Grackle
Brown-headed Cowbird
Baltimore Oriole
House Finch
American Goldfinch

OTHER SPECIES KNOWN TO OCCUR ON THE REFUGE

Mammals

Gray bat
Indiana bat
Eastern Pipistrelle
Big Brown bat
Beaver
Raccoon
Gray and Fox squirrels
White-tailed deer
Cottontail rabbits
Coyote

Fish and Crustaceans

Ozark Cavefish (*Amblyopsis rosae*)
Benton cave crayfish (*Cambarus aculabrum*)
Banded Sculpin
Epigean crayfish

Amphibians and Reptiles

Cave Salamander
Grotto Salamander
Rat Snake
Copperhead
Green Treefrog
Northern Spring peeper
Pickerel Frog

Vegetation

Blackjack Oak
Post Oak
Southern Red Oak
White Oak
Black Hickory
Shagbark Hickory
River Birch
American Elm
American Sycamore
Sweetgum
Persimmon
Flowering Dogwood
Eastern Redbud
Poison Ivy
Green brier
Common periwinkle (*Vincia minor*)
Various sedges, grasses and ferns

Appendix J. Budget Requests

REFUGE OPERATING NEEDS SYSTEM (RONS)

RONS Project # (Projects Not Ranked)	Project Title	One-time Cost	Annual Cost
07001	Science-based Inventory and Monitoring of Refuge Flora and Fauna	$20,000	$2,000
07002	Identify Life History and Requirements for *A. rosae* and *C. aculabrum* for the Logan Cave system	$20,000	$5,000
07003	Purchase Night Vision Equipment for Monitoring Threatened and Endangered Species	$10,000	0
07004	Conduct Study to Identify Hibernacula Used by Logan Cave Gray Bat Colony	$ 3,000	$1,000 **
07005	Identify Logan Cave Gray Bat Foraging Areas	$15,000	$5,000
07006	Monitor Micro-climate of Logan Cave	$ 5,000	$ 500
07007	Monitor Water Quality and Quantity of Logan Stream and Spring	$20,000	$5,000
07008	Initiate Sinkhole Stabilization Project	$5,000	$500
07009	Utilize Cave Radiolocation to Map Cave and Surface Relationship	$5,000	0
07010	Purchase Surveillance Equipment for Law Enforcement	$8,000	0
07011	Develop and Print Logan Cave Brochure	$ 3,000	$ 600
07012	Re-establish Refuge Manager Position	$160,000	$89,000
07013	Hire Public Use Specialist	$160,000	$70,000

MAINTENANCE MANAGEMENT SYSTEM NEEDS

SAMMS Project # (Small Construction)	Project Title	Estimated Cost
2007734361	Construct Information Kiosk at Logan Cave NWR	$10,000
will be assigned by Regional Office if funded	Construct Viewing Platform	$20,000

Appendix K. Consultation and Coordination

OVERVIEW

This appendix lists the consultation and coordination that occurred in preparation of this CCP. It lists the meetings that were held with the various agencies, organizations, and individuals consulted in the preparation of the CCP. There were no biological or public use reviews; therefore no biological or public use review teams were formed.

The following meetings, contacts, and presentations were undertaken by the Fish and Wildlife Service during the preparation of the CCP.

The Service formed a planning team to identify the issues and concerns pertinent to refuge management. The team met twice; October 2005 and June 2006. Key tasks of the team involved defining and refining the vision; identifying, reviewing, and filtering issues; outlining the alternatives; and defining the goals, strategies and objectives. In April 2006, the planning team held a public scoping meeting to gain the insights of local citizens and their perceptions of the issues and concerns facing the refuge.

The planning team members included:

- Ben Mense, Refuge Manager (former), Holla Bend/Logan Cave NWRs
- Durwin Carter, Refuge Manager, Holla Bend/Logan Cave NWRs
- Carla Mitchell, Assistant Refuge Manager, Holla Bend/Logan Cave NWRs
- David Kampwerth, Karst Biologist, FWS, Ecological Services, Conway, Arkansas
- Steve Hensley, Refuge Manager, Ozark Plateau NWR
- Tim Snell, Director, Ozark Karst Program, The Nature Conservancy, Fayetteville, Arkansas
- Blake Sasse, Non-Game Mammal Biologist, Arkansas Game and Fish Commission
- Tina Chouinard, Natural Resource Planner, FWS

Jim Besley, GIS Specialist, FWS, Ecological Services, Conway Field Office, Conway, Arkansas, provided Geographical Information Systems, Cartography.

Appendix L. Finding of No Significant Impact

INTRODUCTION

The Fish and Wildlife Service proposes to protect and manage certain fish and wildlife resources in Benton County, Arkansas, through the Logan Cave National Wildlife Refuge. An Environmental Assessment has been prepared to inform the public of the possible environmental consequences of implementing the Comprehensive Conservation Plan for Logan Cave National Wildlife Refuge. A description of the alternatives, the rationale for selecting the preferred alternative, the environmental effects of the preferred alternative, the potential adverse effects of the action, and a declaration concerning the factors determining the significance of effects, in compliance with the National Environmental Policy Act of 1969, are outlined below. The supporting information can be found in the Environmental Assessment, which was Section B of the Draft Comprehensive Conservation Plan for Logan Cave National Wildlife Refuge.

ALTERNATIVES

In developing the Comprehensive Conservation Plan for Logan Cave National Wildlife Refuge, the Fish and Wildlife Service evaluated three alternatives:

> **Alternative 1: No Management Direction**
> **Alternative 2: Current Management Direction** (No Action Alternative)
> **Alternative 3: Optimize Biological Program and Visitor Services** (Preferred Action)

Each alternative is summarized below.

Alternative 1 represents a custodial approach. Refuge management or resource protection would not occur; fish and wildlife populations would not be monitored, habitats would not be managed or monitored, no land protection would occur, and no law enforcement activities would be performed. The Service would probably enter into management agreements with the Arkansas Game and Fish Commission and/or The Nature Conservancy.

Alternative 2 represents no change from current management of the refuge. All refuge management activities would be directed toward achieving the refuge's primary purpose (to properly administer, conserve, and develop the 123-acre area for protection of a unique cave ecosystem that provides essential habitat for the endangered gray bat, endangered Benton cave crayfish, the threatened Ozark cavefish, and other significant cave-dwelling wildlife species). Active habitat and wildlife management would continue to be limited to protection of the cave entrances and limited access to surface and subsurface habitats. Little to no environmental education and wildlife interpretation would occur. No improvements would be made to the exterior for wildlife observation or photography. Under this alternative, the refuge would not seek out partnerships with adjacent landowners nor other state and federal agencies to contribute to the overall natural resource conservation effort in the area. The primary focus under Alternative 3, the preferred action, is to add a staff person and equipment in order to manage, maintain, restore, and protect the refuge's habitats and wildlife species. Intensive biological monitoring for all species of concern will occur. Active habitat management will be implemented to maintain and enhance water quality and quantity within the cave system, the recharge zone (groundwater recharge areas), and waterways within the bat foraging areas through best management practices, easements, and partnerships with private landowners and other federal and state agencies. Continuous groundwater quality monitoring, which is crucial to the existence of the aquatic species utilizing the cave stream and groundwater corridors, will occur. Utilizing various partners, the refuge will develop a small environmental education program, focusing on karst environments. Limited staff- or volunteer-guided wildlife observation and photography and environmental education and interpretation will occur on the surface. The refuge will develop a community-based volunteer program by establishing a Cave Steward or Friends program.

The Service adopted Alternative 3 as the comprehensive conservation plan for guiding the direction of the refuge for the next 15 years. The overriding concern reflected in this plan is that wildlife conservation assumes first priority in refuge management; wildlife-dependent recreational uses are allowed if they are compatible with wildlife conservation. Wildlife-dependent recreation uses (wildlife observation, wildlife photography, and environmental education and interpretation) will be emphasized and encouraged.

SELECTION RATIONALE

Alternative 3 is selected for implementation because it directs the development of programs to best achieve the refuge purpose and goals. Implementing the preferred alternative will result in management based on sound science for the conservation of a structurally diverse and species diverse karst habitat for threatened, endangered, and resident wildlife. A focused effort will be placed on properly administering, conserving, and developing the 123-acre area for protection of a unique cave ecosystem that provides essential habitat for the endangered gray bat, endangered Benton cave crayfish, the threatened Ozark cavefish, and other significant cave-dwelling wildlife species, while contributing to other national, regional, and state goals to protect and restore karst habitats and species. It provides the best mix of program elements to achieve desired long-term conditions. Baseline inventories and monitoring of management actions will be completed to gain information on a variety of species of special concern. Cooperative partnerships will be conducted with universities, Arkansas Game and Fish Commission, and other agencies and individuals to provide biological information to be used in management decisions. When compatible, the wildlife-dependent recreational opportunities for wildlife observation, wildlife photography, and environmental education and interpretation will be provided and enhanced, while achieving the refuge purpose and remaining consistent with existing laws, Service policies, and sound biological principles.

Under this alternative, all lands under the management and direction of the refuge will be protected, maintained, and enhanced to best achieve national, ecosystem, and refuge-specific goals and objectives within anticipated funding and staffing levels. In addition, the action positively addresses significant issues and concerns expressed by the public.

Environmental Effects

Implementation of the Service's management action is expected to result in environmental, social, and economic effects as outlined in the comprehensive conservation plan. Habitat management, wildlife population management, resource protection, and visitor services' activities on Logan Cave National Wildlife Refuge would result in increased protection for threatened and endangered species; enhanced wildlife populations; karst restoration, enhancement and monitoring; and enhanced opportunities for wildlife-dependent recreation and environmental education. These effects are detailed as follows:

1. Alternative C will benefit the recovery of the refuge's threatened and endangered species and is the Service's preferred management action. Under the preferred action, extensive wildlife population monitoring/surveying will occur to assess population status, trends, wildlife habitat associations, and population responses to habitat management. The Benton cave crayfish and Ozark Cavefish populations will be maintained at a minimum of 35 and 40 individuals, respectively. The refuge will

maintain all other populations of karst species, such as pseudoscorpions, isopods, amphipods, beetles, collembolans, and other blind insects adapted to subterranean habitats. The abundance of the grotto salamander will also be monitored.

2. Logan Cave's gray bat population will be maintained or increased by intensive monitoring and enhancing quality habitat for the maternal roost site and foraging areas along Osage Creek. Micro-climate of cave habitat and biological monitoring of Indian bat populations will increase.

3. Refuge land acquisition, reforestation, and protection will benefit the recovery of threatened and endangered species. Land acquisition of tracts adjacent to Service owned lands, lands within the recharge zone and lands along bat foraging areas will be given priority. Conservation easements and leases can be used to obtain interests necessary to satisfy refuge objectives. The Service can negotiate management agreements with local, state, and federal agencies, and accept conservation easements. The primary purpose of this effort will be to work with partners and private landowners to provide a forest system of sufficient size and carrying capacity to reach regional objectives associated with area-sensitive neotropical migratory birds. This will also help protect and enhance foraging the area for the gray bats, especially along Osage creek and its tributaries

4. Inspection and maintenance of enclosures at least twice a year and stabilization of the sinkhole entrance will help stop sediment erosion caused by foot traffic. Water quantity and quality will be continuously monitored and maintained at a level to achieve refuge purposes. Sensitive aquatic species in the pool will be identified and protected.

5. Habitat restoration and management, along with a focus on accessibility and facility developments, will result in improved wildlife-dependent recreational opportunities. While public use will result in some minimal, short-term adverse effects on wildlife, user conflicts may occur at certain times of the year. These effects will be minimized by site design, time zoning, and implementing refuge regulations. Anticipated long-term impacts to wildlife and wildlife habitats of implementing the management action are positive. In the long run, wildlife habitat and increased opportunities for wildlife-dependent recreation opportunities could result in an increase in economic benefits to the local community.

Potential Adverse Effects and Mitigation Measures

Alternative 3, the preferred alternative, also has some unavoidable impacts. These impacts are expected to be minor and/or short-term in duration. However, the refuge will attempt to minimize these impacts whenever possible. The following sections describe the measures the refuge will employ to mitigate and minimize the potential impacts that could result from implementation of the preferred alternative.

WATER QUALITY FROM SOIL DISTURBANCE AND USE OF HERBICIDES

Soil disturbance due to trail maintenance and the construction of an observation deck are expected to be minor and of short duration. To further reduce potential impacts, the refuge will use best management practices to minimize the erosion of soils as well as seasonal restrictions.

Public use will be very limited and foot traffic will have a negligible impact on soil erosion. To minimize the impacts from public use, the refuge will include informational signs that request trail users to remain on the trails in order to avoid causing potential erosion problems.

Due to the proximity of the cave and potential for adverse effects on aquatic cave species, no herbicides will be used for exotic plant control. Any removal of exotic plants on refuge property will be done by hand.

WILDLIFE DISTURBANCE

Disturbance to wildlife is an unavoidable consequence of any public use program, regardless of the activity involved. While some activities, such as wildlife observation, may be less disturbing than others, all of the public use activities proposed will be planned to avoid unacceptable levels of impact.

The known and anticipated levels of disturbance are not considered to be significant. Nevertheless, the refuge will manage public use activities to reduce impacts. Any future hunting opportunities will also be managed with restrictions that ensure minimal impact on other resources. General wildlife observation may result in minimal disturbance to wildlife. If the refuge determines that impacts from the expected visitor uses are above the levels that are anticipated, those uses will be discontinued or have additional restrictions.

VEGETATION DISTURBANCE

Negative impacts could result from the creation, extension, and maintenance of trails that require the clearing of nonsensitive vegetation along their length. This is expected to be a minor short-term impact.

USER GROUP CONFLICTS

Logan Cave's resources are too sensitive to allow general public use, therefore public programs will not occur on the refuge without supervision or attendance of refuge staff. Since all activities will be planned and prearranged, the only conflicts will be between trespassers and law enforcement officials.

EFFECTS ON ADJACENT LANDOWNERS

Implementation of the preferred alternative is not expected to negatively affect the owners of private lands adjacent to the refuge. Positive impacts that will be expected include higher property values, less intrusion of invasive exotic plants, and increased opportunities for viewing wildlife.

LAND OWNERSHIP AND SITE DEVELOPMENT
Potential development of access roads and visitor parking areas and habitat management could lead to minor short-term negative impacts on plants, soil, and some wildlife species. When site development activities are proposed, each activity will be given the appropriate National Environmental Policy Act consideration during pre-construction planning. At that time, any required mitigation activities will be incorporated into the specific project to reduce the level of impacts to the human environment and to protect fish and wildlife and their habitats.

As indicated earlier, one of the direct effects of site development is increased public use; this increased use may lead to littering, noise, and vehicle traffic. While funding and personnel resources will be allocated to minimize these effects, such allocations make these resources unavailable for other programs.

The management action is not expected to have significant adverse effects on wetlands and floodplains, pursuant to Executive Orders 11990 and 11988.

COORDINATION

The management action has been thoroughly coordinated with all interested and/or affected parties. Parties contacted include:

Congressional representatives
Governor of Arkansas
Arkansas Game and Fish Commission
Arkansas State Historic Preservation Officer
Local community officials
Interested citizens
Conservation organizations

FINDINGS

It is my determination that the management action does not constitute a major federal action significantly affecting the quality of the human environment under the meaning of Section 102(2)(c) of the National Environmental Policy Act of 1969 (as amended). As such, an environmental impact statement is not required. This determination is based on the following factors (40 C.F.R. 1508.27), as addressed in the Environmental Assessment for the Logan Cave National Wildlife Refuge:

1. Both beneficial and adverse effects have been considered and this action will not have a significant effect on the human environment. (Environmental Assessment, pages 59-64)

2. The actions will not have a significant effect on public health and safety. (Environmental Assessment, page 61)

3. The project will not significantly affect any unique characteristics of the geographic area, such as proximity to historical or cultural resources, wild and scenic rivers, or ecologically critical areas. (Environmental Assessment, pages 59-64)

4. The effects on the quality of the human environment are not likely to be highly controversial. (Environmental Assessment, pages 59-64)

5. The actions do not involve highly uncertain, unique, or unknown environmental risks to the human environment. (Environmental Assessment, pages 59-64)

6. The actions will not establish a precedent for future actions with significant effects nor do they represent a decision in principle about a future consideration. (Environmental Assessment, pages 59-64)

7. There will be no cumulatively significant impacts on the environment. Cumulative impacts have been analyzed with consideration of other similar activities on adjacent lands, in past action, and in foreseeable future actions. (Environmental Assessment, pages 62-64)

8. The actions will not significantly affect any site listed in, or eligible for listing in, the National Register of Historic Places, nor will they cause loss or destruction of significant scientific, cultural, or historic resources. (Environmental Assessment, pages 59-64)

9. The actions are not likely to adversely affect threatened or endangered species, or their habitats. (Environmental Assessment, pages 59-64)

10. The actions will not lead to a violation of federal, state, or local laws imposed for the protection of the environment. (Environmental Assessment, pages 59-64)

SUPPORTING REFERENCES
U.S. Fish and Wildlife Service. 2008. Draft Comprehensive Conservation Plan and Environmental Assessment for Logan Cave National Wildlife Refuge, Benton County, Arkansas. U.S. Department of the Interior, Fish and Wildlife Service, Southeast Region.

DOCUMENT AVAILABILITY
The Environmental Assessment was Section B of the Draft Comprehensive Conservation Plan for Logan Cave National Wildlife Refuge and was made available in January and February 2008. Additional copies are available by writing: Holla Bend National Wildlife Refuge, 10448 Holla Bend Road, Dardanelle, AR 72834.

_____   8-8-08
Acting Sam D. Hamilton   Date
Regional Director